Brad thinks I'm NUTS!

Because I learned to use my PSYCHIC powers

Steven Ware Smith

Copyright © 2020 by Steven Ware Smith.

All rights Reserved. No part of this book may be reproduced in any manner without the written permission of the author.

Back cover art, *We Are All Connected*, © Craig W.S. McMaster. Used with permission.

GRATITUDE

I want to extend special thanks to Jerry D. Harthcock, who got me started on my path of spiritual awakening, and assisted and encouraged me along the way.

Special thanks also to my Controlled Remote Viewing (CRV) instructors Lori Williams of Intuitive Specialists, Paul Smith of Remote Viewing Instructional Services, and Joe McMoneagle of The Monroe Institute. Their care and attention during their courses enabled me to make astounding discoveries about my latent psychic abilities.

Download Your FREE "Brad Thinks I'm NUTS!" ESP-Experiment Checklist Now.

www.YouCanLearnTheTruth.com/FreeChecklist

SURPRISE!

To thank you for buying my book, I'd like to give you a very special gift that will help you activate your latent psychic abilities.

My new **ESP-Experiment Checklist** will help you put the information in this book to work for you.

With the Checklist in hand, you'll be able to prepare for and conduct a scientifically controlled ESP (telepathy) experiment with a few close friends in the comfort of your own home.

The Checklist includes…

- A list of materials you will need.
- Instructions on how to structure the experiment to ensure no information can be communicated between the participants by ordinary physical means.
- Instructions on how to properly prepare the "*set and setting*" for the experiment. That includes…
  - ➢ Ways to ensure your participants are in the right *mindset*. An example of a successful ESP experiment is provided on my website to help open the minds of your participants to the possibility they can succeed; and
  - ➢ Instructions on how to establish an *environment* free of distractions.

Download the Checklist right now, BEFORE you start reading.

www.YouCanLearnTheTruth.com/FreeChecklist

CONTENTS

Gratitude iii

Chapter 1: It's Science, Not Séance 1
Chapter 2: What? A Skeptical Engineer Is Teaching Psychic Functioning? ... 8
Chapter 3: The Benefits Of Expanded Consciousness Are Out Of
  This World 22
Chapter 4: Negative, Limiting Beliefs Can Hold You Back 37
Chapter 5: If You Think ESP Is Strange, Take A Look At Modern Physics. 45
Chapter 6: Get Your Mind Right! 58
Chapter 7: The ESP Experiment That "Opened The Door" For Me 64
Chapter 8: Take Off The Blinders And Do Your Own ESP Experiment! ... 73
Chapter 9: How To Remote View—Your Mind Can Perform Miracles! 83
Chapter 10: What The Heck Is *Controlled* Remote Viewing (CRV)? 94
Chapter 11: A Deeper, Really Cool Look At CRV Stages 1-3 104
Chapter 12: Scientific Theories Explaining Psychic Functioning 123
Chapter 13: Where Can You Go From Here? 135

Epilogue 139
Epilogue 2 141
Bibliography 145
About the Author 149

CHAPTER 1

It's Science, Not Séance

Congratulations on taking this step toward expanded consciousness. If you're reading this book, you have a more open mind than my skeptical brother, Brad, who I'm sure you know by now, thinks I'm nuts!

Don't get me wrong. Brad's not a bad guy. I like him. He's a good-hearted soul. But like many people, he's walking around with blinders on. He doesn't realize that being psychic is just another part of being human. Like everyone else (including you!) he has psychic powers. They're just latent because he hasn't learned to recognize them or use them. And in his case, he doesn't want to.

When I was writing this book, I asked him what I could say in the book description to make him read it. His answer? "Nothing. I would *never* read that book." I think that's sad because if he doesn't open his mind to new possibilities, he will never live up to his full potential.

But I know exactly where he's coming from. As far as his beliefs about psychic or nonphysical communications, he's where I was twenty-four years ago—a total skeptic. That's when I got new information through a surprisingly successful extrasensory perception (ESP) experiment a friend of mine convinced me to try. But without that kind of personal experience, it's natural to be skeptical about things you can't sense with your five physical senses. If I had never done that ESP experiment, I would not have done twenty-four years of psychic research and experimentation. Brad and I would probably be in total agreement about those "crazies" who believe in psychic and spiritual experiences.

But relying only on your five physical senses can be misleading. You're drawing conclusions based on incomplete information. Just consider the universe around us. There are things both larger than we can see and smaller than we can see. There are sound frequencies too high for us to hear and too low for us to hear. Does that mean they don't exist?

A few centuries ago, I would have said the astronomer Nikolai Copernicus was nuts for suggesting the sun was the center of our solar system. My opinion would have been that it's intuitively obvious Earth is the center of the universe. Everything goes around the Earth. All you have to do is look up and you can see it for yourself!

Primitive man thought the stars were painted on a shell that rotated around the Earth just beyond their reach. That was the universe. Less than 100 years ago, astronomers thought there was one galaxy in the universe—our Milky Way galaxy—and the entire universe was about 300,000 light-years in diameter. We now know there are at least 100 billion galaxies, and the universe is billions of light-years across.

And what about things too small to see? Before the invention of the microscope around 1600, we had no idea that bacteria caused infections and diseases. We didn't even know they existed. A good many people probably thought God made people sick to punish them for their transgressions. If I had been alive then and someone told me infections and diseases were caused by teeny-tiny little bugs, too small to see, I'm pretty sure I would have thought they were nuts! I would have had to see it to believe it. And if I did see bacteria through a microscope, I would have thought, *Oh, that's how God does it. When we sin, He sends teeny-tiny little bugs to make us sick!*

So it's natural to be skeptical about unseen things, and until 1996, I was certainly skeptical about anything psychic or spiritual. You see, I'm a "science guy." I graduated with honors from the United States Naval Academy with a Bachelor of Science degree in Aerospace Engineering. So in addition to basic sciences like physics and chemistry, I studied things like propulsion systems, aerodynamics, thermodynamics, fluid dynamics, materials, mechanical structures, electrical engineering, differential equations, orbital mechanics, and all the other subjects needed to be an authentic Rocket Scientist! So why am I writing a book like this? That seems the least likely thing a science guy like me would do!

Well, as I mentioned, I participated in a controlled extrasensory perception (ESP) experiment twenty-four years ago to see whether some friends and

I could *mentally* communicate images between us. (I thought it was crazy at the time, but one of those friends dragged me into it.) The results were mind-blowing! The incredible success of that experiment made me realize that, for the first forty-four years of my life, I had been totally blind to the fact that my mind could access information through means other than my five physical senses. I realized I didn't know who I was, *what* I was, or how I fit into the universe.

Following that experience, I studied psychic and spiritual functioning in great detail. I experienced the power of my subconscious mind to communicate with others and to acquire information from distant locations. And I saw other people do these things as well—things I previously believed were impossible! Now, I help curious people experience subconscious communication for themselves. I do this even if they are hard-core skeptics who have never had a psychic or spiritual experience in their lives. There's no magic or woo-woo psychic stuff here. I just teach a straightforward process I've developed over the last twenty-four years.

> Everyone can demonstrate psychic abilities.... You can learn the truth.

The do-it-yourself experiments described in this book are based on solid scientific studies performed by prestigious universities and scientists. The science shows that everyone can demonstrate psychic abilities to some extent, and even the most "un-psychic" get better with training and practice. You can learn the truth.

Some of you, like I was for many years, may be staunch disbelievers in psychic or spiritual functioning. Others may be on the fence. Still others may be believers who want to see what I'm teaching. No matter your current beliefs, I have something of value for all of you in this book.

But before we get into the details, let me tell you what this book is not. This book has nothing to do with the Hollywood version of psychics or mediums. I'm not going to teach you how to make money as a psychic at the county fair, or how to set up shop as a medium channeling the spirits of dead people for grieving relatives. I'm not going to tell you how to meditate to achieve an altered state of consciousness, or how to work with energy centers in your body to achieve a state of well-being. And I'm not trying to leave you with any kind of spiritual or religious awakening, although this book may get you started on that path.

This book will take a much more scientific view of spiritual and psychic functioning. We'll look at real results of scientific studies, and I'll show you some practical, straightforward experiments you can do yourself to discover your own psychic abilities. There will be no magic, no "smoke and mirrors." These abilities will be real. This book is about science, not séance.

Let me give you some background about why I wrote this book. There are two main reasons.

> I was a huge psychic skeptic.

First, growing up, I never had a single psychic or spiritual experience. After studying science and engineering, I became an atheist and a physicalist. I believed the physical universe evolved following the laws of physics and that was all there is. If you couldn't see, hear, smell, taste, or feel it, it didn't exist. I now know, through personal experience, that that's not true. My experiences have opened up a whole new world—no, a whole new *universe*—to me. It's been an extraordinary journey—one that no one should miss. But I know there are millions of people out there who believe like I used to believe, and I want to help those people discover the truth as well.

My second reason for writing this book is to try to improve the sad state of the world we live in. What role can I play in creating a shift to a more conscious world? It seems like humanity is going down a path of increasing hatred and violence. The philosopher Ken Wilbur says 60-70% of people in the world are still in an ethnocentric stage of growing up. That means they are still of the mindset that their particular group—whether it's their religion, their country, their region, their political party, or other affiliation—is correct in its beliefs and everyone else is wrong. They lash out at other groups, causing hatred, discontent, and wars.

In my opinion, it's a false sense of separateness that causes fear, hatred, and violence in the world. Our physical senses continually tell us that we are separate from the other people and objects around us, and our conscious minds don't want to let go of that perception. It's my hope and belief that once you experience for yourself how you're mentally connected to others, you'll be motivated to continue your studies of expanded consciousness, just like I was. In this way, we can grow into a more world-centric stage where everyone realizes we're all in this together and we're all equal. I hope this book helps to create a shift toward a more peaceful, caring world.

Keep in mind, this book provides an *introduction* to psychic and spiritual functioning. It's designed for the curious person who has never had a psychic or spiritual experience. I'm going to show you how to do some basic experiments with a few friends in the comfort of your own home that should prove to you that psychic functioning is real, and you can do it. But before I do that, I'm going to show you how to get into the right mindset to improve your chances of success. We'll talk about how to get rid of limiting beliefs that may be holding you back. For example, if you have the belief that psychic functioning is impossible, I'll help you get rid of that belief by showing you why it's reasonable to believe in it.

Don't worry—this book is *not* going to cover topics like psychic healing, aura viewing, yoga wisdom, crystal gazing, astrology, channeling, destiny, karma, or any other far-out psychic topics that are difficult for most beginners to believe in. Instead, it will stick to the basic goal of showing you how to have your first psychic experience. We're going to crack open the door for you the way my ESP experiment cracked open the door for me twenty-four years ago.

With practice, you'll be able to recognize information coming from your subconscious mind. For many of us, this information is so subtle and so fleeting, we don't consciously perceive it—yet it holds immense value in enabling us to live better, fuller lives.

You can be a happy, prosperous, successful, creative person who has profound spiritual experiences that fill your life with excitement, joy, and love. Learn to use the power of your subconscious mind and these things will come to you. But first, you have to recognize that you *have* a subconscious mind, and it is working continuously to provide you with everything you need. This book is designed to get you started on that path.

Pay attention to the first few chapters of this book, even if they just seem like background information. These chapters are designed to give you the information and mindset you need in order to achieve success in the experiments I describe later.

If you follow the recommendations made in this book, you'll gain a new appreciation of how much the human mind can actually do. If you continue to practice the techniques I'll show you, you'll gain a new appreciation for life and how you as an individual human are connected to everyone and everything.

> You've already done harder things in your life.

Now you might say, "Wow—that's quite an objective!" But achieving this goal is entirely possible if you carefully follow the instructions I provide and *practice*. Hey, you've already done harder things in your life. If you could learn algebra, geometry, and trigonometry as a teenager well enough to graduate high school, you can certainly do this. Even if, like me, you have to look up those courses to even remember what they were about!

(Also, if you're like me and you *do* look them up, you'll probably be flooded by waves of bad memories. *How could I forget how awful high school was?* So maybe you shouldn't look them up. Just remember—*you passed!* You did it! And that's the important thing.)

So now that your confidence has been built up, here are the highlights of what this book covers:

1. I'll give you a little background about me and the experiences that brought me to this point. Believe me, I began this journey as the world's biggest skeptic, but I decided to study psychic functioning with an open mind. I figured, as a science guy, it was the least I could do.
2. I'll cover what you can gain from this book. Hopefully, that will provide you with the motivation needed to see it all the way through, and then some. In the words of my favorite space-traveling toy, Buzz Lightyear, I hope you'll want to go "to infinity and beyond!"
3. For those of you who are physicalists—I know you're skeptical about psychic experiences. I know how you think, because I was one of you. So we'll then take a brief look, without getting too technical, at what today's physicists believe. Once you see the weirdness of modern physics, you'll realize that believing in psychic abilities is not any weirder, especially when those abilities are demonstrated under scientifically controlled conditions.

4. I'll describe a technique for clearing out any negative beliefs you may have that could hinder your ability to demonstrate psychic functioning.
5. I'll describe for you the simple ESP experiment I mentioned earlier, which I participated in back in 1996. Two of my friends and I made some simple drawings out of sight of the others and then attempted to describe each other's drawings without seeing them. I'll tell you how I was *dragged* into that, thinking it was *crazy*, and I'll explain the setup and show you the actual drawings my friends and I made during that experiment—which was, in the end, successful. (It was so incredible, I kept those drawings all these years.) This is the experiment that cracked open the door for me. It showed me that extra-sensory communication is not only possible, it's *real*.
6. I'll show you how to prepare for and conduct an ESP experiment yourself in the comfort of your own home.
7. I'll show you how to prepare for and conduct a simple remote viewing experiment that takes the ESP experiment to the next level. Instead of describing another person's drawing, you'll describe a physical object that person has in their possession.
8. I'll introduce you to Controlled Remote Viewing, or CRV, which is a highly successful protocol that was developed by the military intelligence agencies in the US to train psychic spies during the Cold War. CRV was once a top-secret program but has been declassified, and courses teaching the CRV protocol are now available to civilians like us. I'll show you some samples of actual sessions I did during my CRV training, and I'll give you some recommendations for CRV instructors whom you can trust.
9. For those who are curious about how psychic functioning works, I'll briefly describe some of the latest theories put forth by experts in the field.
10. For those of you who want to pursue expanded consciousness further, I'll provide you with some recommended next steps forward.

In the next chapter, I'll tell you how this skeptical rocket scientist discovered his subconscious mind and became a true believer in psychic functioning.

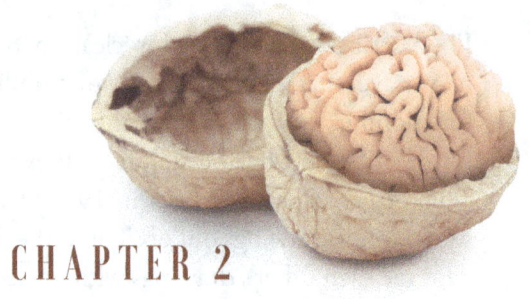

CHAPTER 2

What? A Skeptical Engineer Is Teaching Psychic Functioning?

I'm a science and engineering guy through and through, and grew up being the world's greatest skeptic about psychic or spiritual functioning. How could I possibly be teaching psychic and spiritual functioning now? Well, it was a pretty wild ride, and hopefully, my journey from the world's biggest *skeptic* to a spiritual *believer* to a spiritual *knower* will give me a bit of credibility. It will also show you that everything in this book is based on personal experience *and* solid, scientific evidence. I'm not passing on what other people have experienced unless they also used good scientific controls in their experiments to prevent information from being transferred from one person to another by known methods such as studying body language, eye movements, eye dilation, respiration rate, or a person's response to suggested information.

I was raised in Dallas, Texas in what you would probably call a middle-class family—we weren't poor, but we weren't rich either. My father sold highway construction equipment and traveled to construction sites Monday through Thursday most weeks. I had an older brother and a younger sister, and when my sister entered first grade my mother went back to work to help out with the family finances. Over the years, my mother worked as a bank teller and then a private-school secretary while she took college courses to earn a degree in nutrition. She was studying late at night on really hard courses like organic chemistry. After I was grown and gone, she graduated and became a hospital nutritionist. I was so proud of her for seeing it through.

> Growing up, I never had a single psychic or spiritual experience.

When I was very young, we lived in a suburb of Dallas where we attended a Methodist church and I sang in the children's choir. When I was in the second grade, we moved into town, and my parents decided to join a nearby Presbyterian church. They hauled us kids to Sunday school and church every week. I listened to Bible stories and sermons and played on the church baseball team. But I never felt anything spiritual.

Generally, Presbyterian church services are not very exciting. Everyone sits stoically in the pews without making a sound. There are no "Hallelujahs!" or "Praise the Lords!" coming from that congregation no matter what the minister says. Presbyterians jokingly refer to themselves as "The Frozen Chosen." Many aren't even comfortable shaking hands with fellow members of the church when told to show each other a sign of peace, and holding hands with a stranger during the benediction is a real challenge. It's definitely the right church for introverts, but it was the wrong church for me. The service lasted an hour, but it seemed like days to me. I couldn't wait to get out of there!

At the age of thirteen, I went through the motions of joining the church because my parents wanted me to do it. They were happy for me, but in all honesty, it didn't mean much to me. I felt like I was faking it when I recited the confession of faith. I didn't really believe the stuff in "The Apostles' Creed" but I said it anyway so my parents would leave me alone.

The year before I joined the church, my parents sent me to a week-long church summer camp deep in the hill country of central Texas. We hiked, shot archery, rode horses, and learned how to paddle and steer canoes on the nearby Canyon Lake. We ate our meals on big, long wooden tables that would fill your forearms with splinters if you weren't careful. At night, after supper, counselors would tell us Bible stories before sending us off to our bunkhouses to sleep.

One night after supper, toward the end of the week, we sat around a campfire, under the stars. We were miles and miles away from the lights of any towns, and the Milky Way was emblazoned across the dark sky. It was a beautiful and moving sight. A preacher sat on one side of the crackling campfire, we kids sat on the other, and he preached to us. I could feel the heat of the fire on my face as he told us Bible stories about Jesus and Lazarus and Nicodemus. Occasionally, the wind would shift and engulf me in smoke from the juniper branches we were burning. I kind of welcomed the smoke because it gave me an excuse to momentarily turn away from the fire and give my roasting face a break!

The preacher began talking about Nicodemus needing to be born again. I knew that story, but found it kind of interesting that the preacher referred to him as "Nicodemus the Unborn." That should have given me a clue as to what was coming, but I wasn't astute enough to catch it. All I could think about was that the preacher was wrong, because Nicodemus had to have been born or else he wouldn't have *been* there to talk to Jesus in the first place. Suddenly, the preacher ended his sermon and invited us to come and stand by him if we were ready to be "born again." Ready to be *saved*!

I was startled. I hadn't expected this. I didn't feel moved to go stand next to him. I knew all the stories the preacher had told, and they hadn't had any special effect on me. So I planned to remain seated. I figured one or two kids might go to him, but the rest of us would stay seated. But to my amazement, *all* the other kids got up and rushed to him. When the only other kid left with me got up with tears in her eyes and rushed toward the preacher, I went with her, just to avoid the embarrassment of being the only kid still sitting on that side of the fire.

I felt alone in the middle of this crowd of kids. Friends I had made this week were suddenly like strangers again. They were joyous and happy, and I was faking it. I looked closely at a couple of boys I had become good friends with to see if I could tell whether they were genuinely happy. Were they faking it too? I hoped so; I didn't want to be alone. But to my disappointment, they seemed genuinely happy and convinced that Jesus had talked to them. Why would Jesus talk to them and not to me?

When I think back to that night around the campfire, I wonder how different things would have been if I knew how to listen. Instead of concentrating on the crackling fire, embers shooting into the air, my burning face, and smoke in my eyes, what if I had really listened to the Bible stories while sitting back and gazing at the splendor of the Milky Way? What would I have experienced? If I had paid attention, would I have seen the signs? As insignificant as I appeared to be in the grand scheme of things, God arranged for me to be sitting around that campfire that night. Maybe I would have heard what the other kids heard, and my life would have been very different.

But in any case, it was clear to me that I just wasn't a spiritual person. Any religious beliefs I had were purely rooted in logic. The way I figured it, it made sense to believe in God even if there wasn't any real evidence he existed. When you die, there are only two possibilities: you either cease to exist or you live on as a soul. If you cease to exist, it doesn't matter whether you believed in God or not. You're gone. So you don't lose anything by believing. But if you live on as a soul, you're better off believing so that you can go to heaven rather than hell. So it was logical to believe.

I muddled along with my logical religious belief and a profound lack of spirituality through high school and into my adult life. In high school, I did pretty well academically, particularly in math and science. My parents were proud of me and talked about sending me to a private school, though they never did. I attended public schools in Dallas where I served on the student council, played varsity tennis, and participated in several academic clubs. I had always been interested in airplanes, and wanted to learn how to fly. I read about military flying and became interested in flying fighter jets, so I applied for an appointment to the United States Naval Academy in Annapolis, Maryland. Some people wondered why I didn't also apply to the Air Force Academy, but for me, the Air Force Academy was too new. It had graduated its first class only eleven years earlier in 1959, so it didn't have a long history of traditions. My reading about military flying had instilled in me a respect for military history. I wanted to attend a school full of tradition.

I wasn't sure I would be accepted by the Naval Academy because their requirements were very strict. I had done okay in high school, but overall, I did not graduate in the top ten percent of my class. I was relying on my good math and science grades along with my extracurricular activities to impress the Academy admissions board. So I had a backup plan to attend Texas A&M University if I didn't get in. Texas A&M had lots of tradition, having been established in the 1870s with an all-male student body and the requirement that all students participate in military training. In the 1960s, women were admitted and the military requirement was dropped, but A&M still had a large and famous Reserve Officer Training Corps (ROTC) program where I could join the Air Force ROTC. That way, my dream of flying fighter jets could be kept alive.

I was very excited when I received a last-minute appointment to the Naval Academy. On June 28, 1970, my parents drove me to Love Field airport in Dallas, put me on a plane to Baltimore, and said, "See ya!" There's nothing like being kicked out of the nest to get you motivated! Somehow I found my way from Baltimore to the Naval Academy, found a place to stay that night with some fellow classmates from around the country, and was sworn into the U.S. Navy the next day as a Midshipman.

For my first year and a half at the Academy, attendance at chapel was mandatory. Every Sunday morning, I got up, put on my dress uniform, lined up in formation with my fellow Midshipmen, and marched through throngs of tourists to the beautiful Naval Academy Chapel. There, I listened to sermons, looked at the colorful stained glass windows, and solemnly sang the Navy Hymn—*Eternal Father Strong to Save*. But mostly, I worried about everything else I had to get done that day. We were extremely pressed for time at the Academy, and nearly always sleep-deprived, so I wished I could use that Sunday morning time for something "productive."

I never felt anything spiritual.

Then, halfway through my sophomore year, the U.S. Supreme Court ruled that mandatory chapel at the military academies was unconstitutional. So the 127-year tradition of mandatory chapel at the Academy ended. They still made us get up on Sunday mornings, put on our uniforms, and line up in formation for the tourists, but then we were dismissed. Going to chapel was optional.

Since I felt there were better uses for my time, I never went to chapel again.

I graduated in the top ten percent of my Naval Academy class with a Bachelor of Science degree in Aerospace Engineering. After a short assignment with an operational squadron, I reported to basic flight school in Pensacola, Florida. I was finally ready to start learning how to fly, and was excited beyond belief!

To my shock and dismay, however, the medical staff there diagnosed me with thyroid cancer before I even had my first training flight! I was removed from flight status and had my thyroid surgically removed. As a result, the flight surgeon in charge of medicine at the Naval Aviation Schools Command classified me as Not Physically Qualified (NPQ) for aviation. Thus, I was scheduled to be reassigned to another branch of the Navy.

Well, I didn't take that lying down! I had no desire to serve on a surface ship or submarine—I had seen enough of those things during my summer training at the Academy. I fought the flight surgeon's decision and drafted a letter to the Bureau of Medicine (BUMED) in Washington, D.C., requesting a waiver to continue flight training. I laid out my qualifications and poked lots of holes in the flight surgeon's argument for grounding me. The flight surgeon, a Navy Commander, scoffed at the idea. His attitude was like, "I know what I'm doing and you're just a brand new Ensign. Go ahead and try. You'll never get your waiver."

While I awaited BUMED's decision, I was assigned to tutor incoming flight students who failed one or more of the math tests that every student had to pass to enter the flight training program. I had scored high on those tests, so the officers in charge figured it was a good use of my skills while I was grounded.

Finally, after six months of tutoring my fellow students and searching the mailbox every day, I arrived home one evening and found that the much-anticipated letter from BUMED had arrived. With great trepidation, I tore open the envelope. Inside was a one-sentence letter that merely said, "Duty involving flying in an operational and training status: GRANTED."

Yahoo! I couldn't believe the brevity of the response. They didn't explain their decision at all because they didn't have to. My letter had done all the explaining that needed to be done.

The next morning, I presented BUMED's waiver letter to my *shocked* flight surgeon. I can still see his jaw hitting the surface of his desk! Two days later, orders in hand, I reported to my basic flight training squadron.

> I flew fighter jets for both the Navy and the Air Force, and then served as an intelligence officer in the Reserves.

I graduated first in my class in basic flight training and went on to jet training in Kingsville, Texas. There, I again graduated number one in my class and chose to fly A-7E tactical bombers. Over the next few years, I was assigned to fly off of the aircraft carriers *USS Independence* and *USS Eisenhower* during extended deployments to the North Atlantic and political hot spots in the Mediterranean Sea. Following my sea duty, I was selected to represent the Navy in an exchange tour flying A-10 fighters with the Air Force's 23rd Tactical Fighter Wing for two and a half years. This wing was descended from the 23rd American Volunteer Group—the so-called "Flying Tigers" of World War II. We still had the Flying Tiger logo and the shark's teeth painted on our planes. Very cool!

I served on active duty a total of eight years after graduation and then served fourteen years in the reserves as an intelligence officer.

> I worked as an engineer for a major defense contractor working on radar systems, then went to law school, became a patent attorney, and drafted high-technology telecommunications patents for 26 years.

When I left active duty in 1982, I had several job offers. I chose to take a position as an engineer working on an Over-The-Horizon (OTH) radar system with General Electric (GE), a major defense contractor. I was proud of the fact that our OTH radar system made it impossible for the Soviet bomber fleet to launch a surprise attack on North America. What a thrill it was to see the Soviets "throw in the towel" soon after our radar went operational. I was soon recognized not only for my engineering abilities but also for my technical writing abilities and was promoted to engineering manager.

I did well in the radar systems department but resented the constraints on my individuality and the fixed compensation structure of the big corporation, which I felt didn't properly reward initiative, abilities, and dedication. I longed for more. I wanted a job where my rewards were directly proportional to my abilities, the effort I put in, and my results. If I had a major success, I wanted a major reward, not just a step up on the corporate ladder.

GE's corporate Human Resources department classified me as an individual with high potential for upper management in GE, but when I went to my managers and requested assignments in other departments that would give me the experience I would need to successfully move into an upper management position, they refused. They said they needed me right where I was. I was disillusioned, to say the least, and began to investigate alternative careers. After seven years with GE, I left and went to law school at The University of Texas. After graduating and passing the Texas bar exam in 1992, I became a patent attorney where I could combine both my engineering and law degrees doing interesting and important work. After three years of learning the trade in a large law firm, I left and set up my own practice. I was finally my own boss!

It was a great life. It was 1995—twenty-one years after I graduated from the Naval Academy, and I finally had a job where my compensation was directly related to my abilities and how hard I worked. It was interesting work, and I got busy obtaining high-technology patents for individuals, small companies, and major corporations.

One such client was Jerry, a genius at designing microprocessors. I obtained a couple of patents for him on his brilliant processor architectures, and we became friends in the process. He ran his own company with about ten or so electrical engineers and computer scientists as employees.

Everything seemed normal until early 1996 when, as the name of the play says, "a funny thing happened on the way to the forum." I was completely shocked one day when he told me over a lunch of fajitas and enchiladas that he had discovered that if someone drew something on a piece of paper and stared at it, he could close his eyes and meditate for a few minutes, and tell them what it was. He was talking about a type of extrasensory perception (ESP)—telepathy! Reading people's minds! This was something I absolutely did not believe in. I thought he had gone crazy! In fact, I started calling him "Crazy Jerry." He kept pestering me to try it with him, and multiple times I told him to *get lost!*

But he persisted, and I finally gave in and invited him to come to my house and demonstrate his ability to me and my girlfriend, Maria. He came over, and we decided to do an experiment where we took turns trying to describe each other's drawings without physically seeing them. I'll describe the experiment for you in detail in a later chapter, and show you the actual drawings we made.

> **The experiment was an incredible success! It was undeniable that information had somehow been transmitted between us through some unknown means.**

To my utter astonishment, we accurately described the other person's drawing in every session we did; and in two sessions, one of us described the other person's drawing *exactly right*. It was undeniable that information had somehow been transmitted between us through some unknown means—some subconscious mental connection that is not recognized by most conventional modern scientists. The funny thing was, Maria did even better than Jerry, and she had never done it before. His results were good, but hers were absolutely phenomenal!

My materialistic worldview had been shattered. Obliterated. And I had to find a new one. So I started extensively studying psychic research, meditation, and remote viewing. I took several courses and discovered people could be trained to use their psychic abilities. Before long, I was amazing myself with my psychic and spiritual abilities and had not one, but several, life-changing spiritual experiences that I'll describe for you later. I was forty-four years old and had never had a spiritual experience. Now I could do it almost at will!

Each new book or course that I discovered was just enough of an advance that I could accept it. Some of the stuff that I learned and did a few years down the road, I could never have accepted in the beginning. It was as if some spiritual power was leading me and only feeding me what I could consume at the time.

The first book I read after our ESP experiment was one that Jerry recommended called "Cosmic Voyage" by Courtney Brown, Ph.D., an associate professor of political science at Emory University. Dr. Brown had become interested in what he called Scientific Remote Viewing. It was based on the Coordinate Remote Viewing protocol used by the military for psychic spying during the Cold War. Now called *Controlled* Remote Viewing (CRV), an army intelligence unit had proven its accuracy in many situations over many years.

Dr. Brown had been trained in Scientific Remote Viewing by a former member of that army intelligence unit, and his book described a number of his remote viewing sessions with his instructor monitoring the sessions. Dr. Brown's sessions were performed essentially blind—that is, with no foreknowledge of the "target," that is the remote event, person, or thing he was supposed to describe. I say "essentially blind" because instead of having a theoretically infinite number of possible targets, he and his instructor had agreed on a list of thirty or so targets that would be viewed. Dr. Brown just didn't know which of the thirty targets he was getting in any particular session.

Some of his sessions were kind of weird, such as when the targets were things like UFOs and extraterrestrials. I thought that was unfortunate, because it hurt the credibility of the book and the remote viewing process. The ET thing was enough to put a lot of people off, but it was worse because with those types of targets, referred to as *esoteric* targets, he couldn't get any feedback on how accurate his sessions were. You know what I mean? It's highly unlikely that an alien—a little green man or a "Grey"—is going to show up and confirm that the control panel of his flying saucer looks just like what Dr. Brown described!

The saving grace was that his instructor randomly threw in some real-world targets without warning Dr. Brown, and Dr. Brown accurately described those targets. So in the end, the credentials of Dr. Brown and his instructor and the accuracy of the sessions directed toward the real-world targets gave the book a high degree of credibility in my eyes. It made me want to learn to be a remote viewer.

The most useful thing for my continuing studies was that Dr. Brown laid out a multistage educational program to learn remote viewing. He recommended taking a course in Transcendental Meditation (TM); taking a course called the Gateway Voyage from The Monroe Institute in Virginia; reading several books associated with each of those courses; and taking a remote viewing course given by one of the former members of the Army's psychic intelligence unit.

I did all those... and more.

TM is a mantra-based meditation technique where you mentally repeat a word to yourself over and over to clear out your thoughts. When you quiet the chatter of your conscious mind, you enter a realm of profound silence. At this subconscious level, you can perceive information you never knew was there. In TM, they call it "God-consciousness." TM teaches that you should meditate for twenty minutes twice a day. I took the course and started meditating. The associated books emphasized that if you alternate meditation and activity during your day, you will bring God-consciousness into your life. According to Maharishi Mahesh Yogi, the man who brought TM to the West, when the mind transcends during meditation from the conscious level to the subconscious level, it loses its individuality and becomes omnipresent. When the mind comes back into the field of relative life, it gains individuality again, but it also seems to retain some of the great unbounded universal status it had just attained. With practice, the mind begins to retain more and more of that experience in the activity of daily life. In other words, you begin to live your life in a spiritually awakened state. You see how blinded you were before. It's like you were in prison, but now you are free.

The Gateway Voyage course from The Monroe Institute uses some advanced sound technologies to achieve certain brainwave frequencies and to synchronize your brainwaves on each side of your brain when you listen through headphones. This produces the same brainwave patterns measured on meditating yogis who have practiced meditation for twenty years or more.

If, after reading this book, you are convinced you want to pursue your awakening further, I highly recommend you go to a residential course at The Monroe Institute. It's such a unique place. The Monroe Institute is in a serene country setting where serendipitous things seem to happen.

For example, when I took my Gateway Voyage course there, we had an initial gathering where we all sat with pillows on the floor in the main living room and got a welcome speech from our instructors. They said, "Before we get started, we want you to look around the room at the other participants and find someone you don't know. Find someone who, from their appearance, you think is very different from you. Then take five to ten minutes to go talk to that person."

Well, I looked around the room, and I already knew two or three people because we had met at the airport and had taken the shuttle to the Institute together. I was a tall, thin, middle-aged white guy with short hair. So I looked for someone who was either short and heavy-set or maybe someone of color with long hair. No luck with the short, heavy-set person, but sitting in the back, near a corner—was a young black guy with dreadlocks hanging down to his shoulders. I looked at him and thought, "That's my guy!" So I went over and introduced myself, and we had a good conversation. He was from Belgium and was very nice, and very open. I liked him a lot. I guess that was the purpose of the exercise—to demonstrate that we're all alike more than we're different.

A couple of days later, when we were taking a break, I stepped out the back door and there was a group of guys huddled together at the side of the building, and my dreadlocked friend was one of them.

He called out, "Hey Steven, come here, you have to see this."

The guys had a pair of copper rods with a 90° bend in them. I looked at the rods and said, "Oh no, those are divining rods. I don't believe in that stuff."

So my friend said, "Just hold these in your hands and walk from that corner of the building to that corner," indicating the back wall of the building.

So I did, and when I got about halfway down, the rod tips suddenly moved to point at each other without my doing anything.

"What was that?" I asked. They all laughed and told me that was where the underground water line entered the building going to the kitchen.

So here was a whole new experience I never would have had if I hadn't talked to my dreadlocked friend. That's just the kind of experiences The Monroe Institute gives you. And you'll make new friends from all over the world.

I also read three related books by Robert Monroe: *Journeys Out of the Body*, *Far Journeys*, and *Ultimate Journey*. These books about Robert's out-of-body-experiences (OBEs) were fascinating and very believable because of his engineering background and his writing style, which was to present facts without jumping to conclusions. If you continue your studies, I highly recommend these books.

> I took remote viewing courses from three different former members of the Army's psychic intelligence unit.

Finally, I took not one, but several remote viewing courses from three different former members of the Army's psychic intelligence unit. I'll talk about this in more detail later in the book, but suffice it to say, this was also very successful.

In the end, a completely new reality was opened up for me. The meditation made me aware during the day of little signs attempting to lead me in particular directions. Over time, my intuition greatly improved. I even had a spontaneous OBE myself that proved to me that I was more than my physical body, and convinced me I existed independent of my body. It erased all fear of death. I'll tell you more about this later. And then, to my total surprise, over a period of several years, I made contact with six deceased friends and family members and even helped my father move on in the afterlife using knowledge I learned from The Monroe Institute.

I don't address how to have an OBE or how to communicate with the souls of deceased individuals in this book. Although I have good reasons for believing those types of experiences are real, they are better left for a more advanced book. As I said, this book is about lifting the veil—cracking open the door and getting a peek at some very basic psychic abilities everyone can demonstrate.

> If you want to learn more about my OBE or my communications with those in the afterlife, contact me through my website: www.YouCanLearnTheTruth.com
> I'll send you additional information.

Over time, I began to perceive that all humans communicate with each other at a subconscious level, but most don't realize it. We're so focused on the ego (that conscious part of us that wants to know everything and control everything), that we completely miss the connections we have to other people, to the Earth, and to the universe as a whole. I realized it's this false sense of separateness that causes fear, hatred, and violence in the world. People perceive the world as a place of me-versus-you in a struggle for limited resources. If they fear you are taking their resources or challenging their way of life, they hate you, and violence erupts to correct this wrong. There can be no true peace and well-being in the world so long as there are so many people who feel separate from others and from the Earth itself. The sense of separation drives fear, and fear drives violence.

Through the years that I studied expanded consciousness, I continued drafting high-technology patent applications and prosecuting them through the patent office until I retired from my law practice in 2018. When I looked back over my working years, I was proud that I had always worked in jobs where I could help others and contribute to the greater good. My days in the Navy helped maintain peace during the Cold War. My days at GE helped bring an end to the Soviet Union. And my days as a patent attorney helped bring in the golden age of wireless telecommunications we all enjoy and find so useful in our lives today.

I looked forward to a retirement where I could sleep late, live at a more relaxed pace, and spend quality time with my wife, my kids, and my grandkids. Ah yes—the life of an old retired guy! But these days, retirement can last for 25 or 30 years, and I was already thinking I would be bored or feel guilty for spending so much time concentrating on my own happiness. After all, as I looked at world events, I couldn't help but notice that humanity seemed to be pointed in a negative direction—going down a path of increasing hatred and violence. I was deeply concerned about the state of the world. I contemplated what else I could do to help my fellow man during this next phase of my life.

I decided to do something completely different and totally unexpected—I'll teach people about psychic and spiritual functioning!

So as I retired and contemplated the next phase of my life, I wondered, *Is there anything **I** can do to help people feel more connected?* If I could help people recognize that we are all connected—we're all One—then I could help to reverse the trend of increasing hatred and violence so evident in the world today.

So I wrote this book and created the associated online course, entitled *The Reality of Psychic and Spiritual Experiences: How an Aerospace Engineer Learned the Truth, And How You Can, Too!* I want to help as many people as possible awaken to their greater selves.

As we become more conscious, we naturally become more compassionate, and we begin to live more in service to others and the Earth. But there can be no planet-wide awakening or real behavior shift without *all* of us, including *you*. And that's why I'm so glad you're taking that most important first step by reading this book.

If there's anything I've learned through all this, it's that you don't have to be a natural-born psychic to develop these abilities. You can be trained to do them. I'm the perfect example. Believe me, if *I* can be trained to do them, *anybody* can be trained to do them.

And that includes *you*!

In the next chapter, we'll look a little deeper at what you can achieve with the desire and, of course, practice.

CHAPTER 3

The Benefits Of Expanded Consciousness Are Out Of This World

In this chapter, I'll talk about the benefits of expanded consciousness. This discussion assumes you are successful with the exercises described in Chapters 8 and 9 and continue with your exploration of expanded consciousness as I recommend in Chapter 13. How will your life be made better when you learn to use the power of your subconscious mind?

But before we get into that, let me first say something about the use of psychedelics—psychoactive drugs like Lysergic Acid Diethylamide (LSD) and psilocybin. LSD was first synthesized in 1938 and popularized by the hippie movement in the 1960s (*Right on! Far out! Groovy!*). Psilocybin is the active chemical in the little brown mushrooms used by the people of Central and South America for thousands of years in sacred religious and spiritual ceremonies—for healing, for divination, and other purposes. (*A walk with the dead, anyone?*)

All kidding aside, I have never used these drugs and don't recommend them even though, prior to their being declared illegal as part of the War on

Drugs, they were given to hundreds of volunteers without incident in clinical studies at New York University, UCLA, and Johns Hopkins.

Initially, the studies involved terminally ill cancer patients who were having problems facing the trauma of imminent death. Many of the volunteer patients reported that over the course of a single guided psychedelic "journey" they reconceived how they viewed their cancer and the prospect of dying. Note I said a *guided* psychedelic journey. Great care was taken to get the patients into the proper mindset and to provide a safe and supportive environment so that no one had a so-called "bad trip." After *one* dosage, several of the patients said they had lost their fear of death completely.

Michael Pollan, a professor of journalism at the University of California at Berkeley, is a bestselling author who examines various aspects of the agricultural industry, the food chain, and man's place in the natural world. In his 2018 book, *How to Change Your Mind: What the New Science of Psychedelics Teaches Us About Consciousness, Dying, Addiction, Depression, and Transcendence*, he describes a later experiment performed at Johns Hopkins in 2006 where thirty *healthy* volunteers who had never before used psychedelics were given a pill containing either a synthetic version of psilocybin or an active placebo, which happened to be Ritalin. A scientific article describing the study reported, "Individuals transcend their primary identification with their bodies and experience ego-free states. They return with a new perspective and profound acceptance." (Griffiths, R.R.; W.A. Richards; U. McCann; and R. Jesse. "Psilocybin Can Occasion Mystical-Type Experiences Having Substantial and Sustained Personal Meaning and Spiritual Significance," *Psychopharmacology* 187, no. 3 (2006): 268-283. doi: 10.1007/s00213-006-0457-5).

> Note: All of the books, courses, and articles I mention in this book are listed in a bibliography at the end.

The study authors found it was not difficult to tell which volunteers got the psilocybin. The experiment was performed in a chapel, and while the Ritalin volunteers sat quietly in their pews, the psilocybin volunteers wandered around the chapel exclaiming that love was everywhere and everything was love! The monitors even had to lock the doors because one volunteer wanted to run down the street proclaiming the coming of the Messiah! Boy, I would have loved to have been there to see that!

The researchers found that a high dose of psilocybin could be used to safely and reliably trigger a mystical experience—typically described as the dissolution of one's ego followed by a sense of merging with nature or the universe. What was most remarkable about the results reported in the study is that participants ranked their psilocybin experience as one of the most meaningful in their lives, comparable to the birth of their first child or the death of a parent. Two-thirds of the participants rated the session among the top five most spiritually significant experiences of their lives. One-third ranked it *the* most significant spiritual experience of their lives.

Despite this, as I noted earlier, I have never used these drugs and don't recommend them. You may ask, if psychedelics are that effective, why don't I recommend them? Well, the answer is threefold.

1. They are still highly illegal. Unless you can get into a sanctioned study, or live in one of the few localities where they are approved for medical use, you'd have to get them illegally and would not be sure what you're getting or its purity or dosage. That could make them extremely dangerous.

Don't let this be you!

2. Even though others have reportedly used them without ill effect, I kind of like my brain the way it is. I'd rather not chance it. With my luck, I'd be the first subject who ever experienced brain damage from a "safe" dosage. Or one who went on a trip and never came back!
3. Most importantly, I don't recommend them because you can achieve the same results without them. It'll take longer than an afternoon, but you can achieve a great deal within six to nine months using the techniques I'm going to describe for you.

Alright, so how will you benefit if you follow the recommendations in this book? In a word, I'd say it's *empowerment*. When you have gathered together a group of friends and completed the experiments I describe, you will almost surely have experienced that you have a connection at a subconscious level to information that is not attainable with the five physical senses. You will know that you have subconscious connections to other people. And your eyes will be opened to the fact that you have abilities most people don't even dream they have.

If that piques your curiosity like it did mine, and you continue to study expanded human consciousness, here are some other benefits that *I* saw, and I'm convinced *you* can see within just a few months.

Within just two or three months of starting my meditation practice, I became aware during the day of...well, I'd call them "little signs", which were attempting to lead me in particular directions.

What do I mean by that? Well, there was a scene in the movie *Sleepless in Seattle* where Meg Ryan has sent Tom Hanks a letter inviting him to meet her at the top of the Empire State Building on Valentine's Day. Tom hasn't taken the letter seriously even though his son, Jonah, has. Some of Tom's friends are trying to hook him up with another woman, and have invited him on a blind date to go sailing with them. As Tom approaches the front of the marina, he notices a bus go by with a big banner on its side advertising New York City. Sign number 1. He goes into the building and as he's walking through a waiting area, a young girl walks by him in the opposite direction wearing one of those T-shirts that says "I ♥ N Y." Sign number 2. He turns and stares at her as she walks away. By the time he reaches the dock, the signs are too much and he calls off the sailing date!

That's the kind of signs I was getting. Sometimes the sign was so obvious—so in-your-face—that I literally stopped what I was doing and looked up and said, "That was way too obvious. You need to be more subtle!"

One experience occurred late on a Friday afternoon when I was in my office in a large law firm in Dallas. I was looking forward to getting out of there for the weekend. I took a file out to my secretary and noticed an issue of the Dallas Bar Association's *Headnotes* newsletter, laying on a nearby counter. I picked it up and scanned a few headlines and saw that the Intellectual Property Law section was presenting a Continuing Legal Education (CLE) class about patent law that evening. "Ugh!" I thought. "Who would schedule a CLE class on Friday evening?" I decided I wouldn't go and walked down the hall to get a bottle of water out of the refrigerator in the breakroom. While I was there, I overheard two associates talking about the class and heard one of them mention that the class included dinner. So now the class was much more appealing. I walked back to my secretary's desk and looked at the newsletter again. Sure enough, right there in the announcement about the class, it said dinner would be served. I had completely missed that the first time I read it. I decided to go.

So there were two signs telling me to go to this CLE class. First was the newsletter, conveniently placed where I would see it. Second was the conversation I overheard in the breakroom, which made me change my mind about not going. And what was the result? I met my future law partner at that class. We sat together at the dinner, and she convinced me I could make more money and enjoy my practice more if I left the big law firm and "hung out my own shingle." I did, and we later decided to join our practices. Not only that, a couple of years later, she introduced me to the woman who would eventually become my wife. Little signs showing me the way.

Sometimes, however, I decide not to follow the signs. Like when they are pointing me toward a major decision, and I look for some sort of confirmation but don't get it. One such experience occurred when I got on a plane to fly to Albuquerque on the way to a three-day, CLE conference in Santa Fe, New Mexico. I was in an aisle seat, and a lady and her 10-year-old son were sitting next to me in the middle and window seats, respectively. I got out a book I was reading at the time, which happened to be *Seth Speaks* by Jane Roberts. In this book (and others referred to as *The Seth Material*), Jane channeled information from a spiritual entity named Seth about the nature of reality and our place in it. Jane would go into a trance, and her voice would change to that of Seth. As she spoke, her husband, Robert, wrote down what she said using a form of shorthand and later wrote it out in full sentences for publication. It was a kind of way-out-there book, but I was intrigued by the fact that Seth described, in great detail, a novel explanation of how matter is formed at the quantum level when Jane had no science education whatsoever.

As an aside, I noticed that much of what Seth said in this book about the nature of the spiritual realm coincided with the experiences Robert Monroe reported in his trilogy of books about his OBEs, although the two authors used different terminology. For example, Seth said we each belong to a "soul group" where each personality in the group reflects a human life we have already lived. Monroe also reported he was part of a group of personalities reflecting lives he had already lived, but he called this group his "I-there" to distinguish it from his earthly consciousness, which he called his "I-here." I pulled information from both *Seth Speaks* and Monroe's OBE books as the basis for the hierarchy of spiritual levels I describe in my novel, *An Adventurous Soul: One soul's exciting journey through the Human Learning School.*

Back on the plane, the lady sitting next to me noticed the book title, *Seth Speaks*, and said, "That's interesting. My son's name is Seth. And we just came from Massachusetts where we went to the museum for the Salem witch trials, and the curator's name was Seth."

That got my antennae up! Seth is a pretty rare name in this day and age, so it was quite a coincidence that as I read *Seth Speaks*, she and her son, Seth, sat next to me, and they had just met another Seth. Now I know what you're thinking: it was just a coincidence—or as we would have jokingly called it as kids—a coinkydink. But I had become aware that coinkydinks like that were often signs for me. As the lady and I talked, she told me she was selling her house outside of Albuquerque. She said it was a beautiful house sitting on a mountainside with a magnificent view of the valley below. She said they were having an open house the following weekend, and she gave me the address and invited me to look at it.

Was I getting a sign that I should buy her house and move to Albuquerque?

The house sounded wonderful, and as it just so happened, the timing was perfect because my situation at the time would easily let me move to Albuquerque if I decided to. Most of my patent work was done long distance via email, so from a work standpoint, it didn't matter where I lived. Socially, I was single and unattached, so moving was not a big problem. I decided I would visit the open house the following Saturday to see if I felt any strong emotions about the house.

My conference was scheduled to end on Friday evening, and I had booked a flight back home out of Albuquerque for Saturday evening so I could do a little sightseeing around New Mexico during the day on Saturday. On a beautiful, bright, clear Saturday morning, I drove north and west from Santa Fe to Bandelier National Monument where I hiked to 11,000-year-old cliff dwellings. I could feel the spiritual energy of the place as I walked. I could picture the valley in my mind as a vibrant hub of activity back before climate change turned much of the southwest United States into a desert and forced the occupants to migrate elsewhere.

But looking at the cliff dwellings, I had to wonder what motivated these people to build their homes in this defensive position? It had to take many years of incredible effort to carve these dwellings out of the sandstone cliffs. The logical conclusion, unfortunately, is war. It seems that even in prehistoric times, people just couldn't get along.

Back in the car, I continued my drive west through the mountains and then drove south through the beautiful Jemez Valley on my way back to Albuquerque. As a result of my conversation with the lady on the plane, I had planned to get back in time to go to the open house.

As I drove up the narrow mountain road and went into the house, I was highly alert to see if I felt a strong positive vibe. I decided I would put in an offer if I did, since the signs were definitely pointing me in that direction. But as it turned out, the house was okay, but I didn't feel anything special about it or the area where it was located. The mountain was not as high as I expected, and the climate was more desert-like than I wanted. So I declared the signs a false alarm, drove back to the airport, and flew home.

It could be that my life would have been 100 percent better if I had moved to Albuquerque. Or it could have been 100 percent worse. Who knows where these signs were trying to lead me? Maybe to a life of suffering. Some people achieve their spiritual goals that way. Personally, I'd rather not!

I still see the signs, or at least some of them, and feel they are trying to lead me to circumstances where I can help other people, which, deep down, I feel is my life purpose. If I ignore the signs or don't even notice them, my impression is that I'm given new signs leading me to similar circumstances. I like being aware of the signs and making conscious decisions to follow them or not, rather than just stumbling along blindly. Maybe you would too.

I also had serendipitous things happen that seemed far more than coincidences. For example, I was at lunch with friends and mentioned that I had developed an interest in studying the limits of human consciousness. A friend, who had never before mentioned any interest in this subject at all, casually said, "There's a book by Doctor Larry Dossey you should read. It's about healing people with prayer. I forget the exact title, but I think it's interesting because he's the head of medicine at Medical City Dallas." I looked up Dr. Dossey and found he wrote *Healing Words: The Power of Prayer and the Practice of Medicine*. I followed up by reading that book and found that it was *exactly* what I needed at that point in my spiritual development—an advance, but not too much for me to accept.

Is this sort of thing the "God-consciousness" the TM books talk about? Is this the Holy Spirit working in my life, as the Bible might say? As a scientist, I say I don't know. The signs and serendipitous happenings are unmistakably there, but I don't know who's leaving or causing them. The signs have never led me to do anything evil, so I continue to welcome them.

So, what else can you expect to gain from reading this book and practicing? Well, within a few months of starting my meditation practice, I learned how to get answers to basic questions like, "What's my true nature?" A pretty basic question I would guess we'd all like to know the answer to.

The Monroe Institute's *Gateway Voyage* course teaches you how to get your mind to what they call various "Focus" levels. For example, Focus 10 is a state where your body is asleep but your mind is awake. At Focus 12, your mind is in a state of expanded awareness while your body remains deeply relaxed and asleep. In this state, as you relax in a deep state of meditation, you can formulate a question in your mind, toss it out to the universe, and silently wait for an answer. To my surprise, the first time I tried it, answers came. Not in words, but in the form of symbols. As I've learned in several later courses, your subconscious mind doesn't communicate using spoken or written language as our conscious mind does. So it gives you a symbol that's meaningful to you.

For example, when I asked the universe, "What's my true nature?" I found myself floating in the blackness of outer space with the front roller of a steamroller coming at me. It hit me and rolled over me. I kind of stuck to it until I was on the backside of it, upside down. I then separated from it and watched it proceed away. I wasn't hurt. I was run over by a steamroller, and I was fine! To me, that symbolized the fact that my true nature is that of an eternal spiritual being. My physical body will die, of course, but my spiritual being cannot be killed. You may have a different interpretation of that vision, but it was *my* symbology. Get your own! *Ha!* Just kidding! Actually, you have your own, and when you discover it, you'll be the only one who can interpret it correctly for you.

Okay, so you can get answers from the cosmos. What else can you expect to gain? Well, my intuition was greatly improved. We all have sleeping intuitive abilities that can be turned into reliable life-enhancing skills. With desire and practice, everyone can improve their intuition. For example, I used to be pretty clueless about other people's intentions when I met them. After learning to recognize intuitive input, I now have a much better feel for whether a person is trustworthy, or whether they're an energy taker or an energy giver. I try to stay away from people who suck energy from those around them. You may not have thought about it in that way, but you probably know someone who is just exhausting to be around. Working with them quickly tires you out, and it's usually a losing proposition. When I sense an energy taker, I run!

> Better intuition can save your life!

I know one elderly lady who has studied and practiced expanded consciousness for many years. One day I asked her what she thought was the most important benefit she had gained, and she said, "Better intuition. It can save your life!" She then told me about the time she was driving on the Interstate behind a big truck that was hauling half of a mobile home. You've seen those, right? They were going up a hill, so the truck started slowing down, and she decided to go around it. But then *something* told her not to, and she hung back instead. Just then, the truck crested the hill and a wind gust caught that mobile home and blew the back end of it completely across the lane where she would have been if she had tried to pass. It would have knocked her car off the highway and into a ditch at seventy miles per hour. That "something" she heard? That's intuition.

I also know a guy who has an aircraft maintenance shop at an airport in East Texas. Here's a diagram showing the layout of the airport.

— Brad thinks I'm NUTS! —

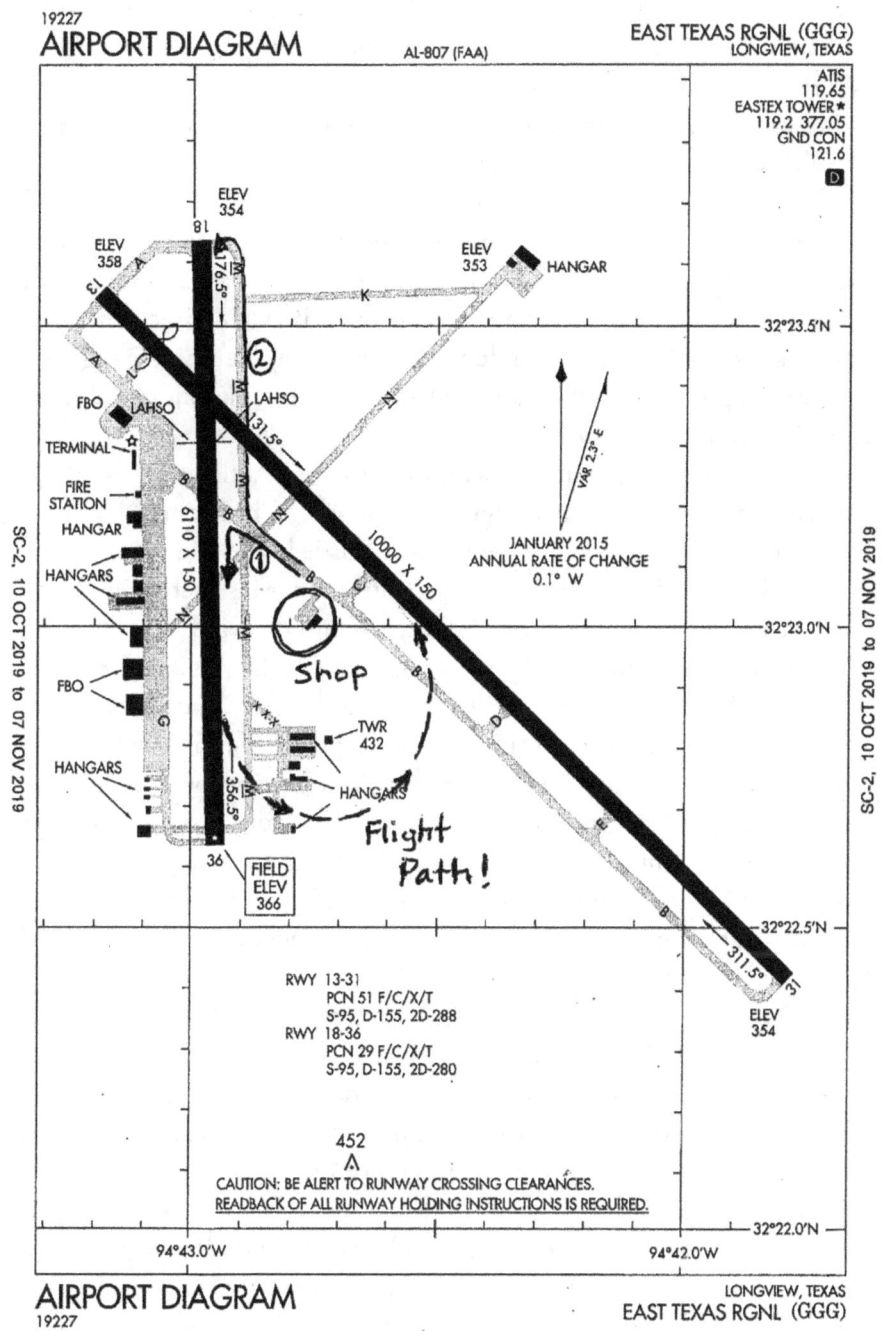

The runways are the thick black lines. As you can see, there's one runway on the left side that runs straight up and down—that's north and south—and there's another runway that intersects it running from the upper left to the lower right—that's northwest to southeast.

I have circled his shop, which is located near the runways off of taxiway "B", called taxiway Bravo in pilot lingo.

Whenever his shop does some maintenance on an airplane, he takes the plane out for a test flight before telling the customer it's ready for pickup. When the north-south runway is being used, he can save a lot of taxiing time by taking off from the intersection where taxiway Bravo intersects the north-south runway. That's about the midpoint of the runway, but there is still plenty of runway length to take off in the small airplanes he works on. I have labeled that taxi route as route 1 on the diagram.

On one particular day, he was taxiing out to do a test flight on a single-engine plane they had put a new engine in. Everything had tested fine during the engine run-ups at the shop, so he wasn't worried. The wind was from the south, so the air traffic controller in the control tower instructed him to take off on the north-south runway headed south—into the wind.

As he taxied up taxiway Bravo toward the runway, he says *a little voice* told him to go full length—that is, go all the way to the north end of the runway, at the top on the diagram, and use the full length of the runway to take off instead of taking off from the intersection. So following route 2, he turned right onto taxiway "M" (that's called taxiway Mike) and taxied up to the north end of the north-south runway. He took off headed south and as he climbed through 700 feet above the ground, which would probably have been about adjacent to his shop, the engine suddenly quit. Deader than a door-nail! His plane was now a glider!

He dropped the nose of the plane to maintain flying speed, and as he descended, he was able to turn to the left and follow the flight path I drew as a dotted line toward the other runway headed northwest. He was rapidly approaching the ground and wasn't sure the plane would make it to the runway, so he kept the landing gear up to reduce drag and increase his gliding distance. When he was about fifty feet from the ground, he saw he was going to make it to the runway, so he put the landing gear handle down. The instant the last wheel locked into the down position, the tires hit the pavement, and he was able to bring the plane to a stop on the runway without a scratch.

He jokingly says the only thing that needed to be cleaned up was his pants!

He was only able to make that turn and safely land that plane because he had taken off from the north end of the north-south runway. If he had done his usual takeoff from the intersection, there's no way he could have made it back, and he would have crashed off the airport.

That "little voice" he heard telling him to go full length? That's intuition. I asked him about it, and he said, "Yeah, I hear that little voice a lot." That's nice to have.

What other abilities could you develop? Well, I had great success in my remote viewing courses. Remote viewing enables you to describe people, places, things, and events from far beyond the range of your physical senses, in the present or other time periods. I'll show you later how I accurately described an event that occurred 900 miles away and 50 years in the past, when all I was told was a reference number and that my target was an event.

What? Wait a minute... Yep, that's right. I'll show you the complete summary I wrote of that session and show you a photo of a clay model I built in the final stage of the remote viewing process. This one totally blew my mind—again!

How about having an out-of-body experience, or OBE? Would that be interesting? Within nine months of the ESP experiment I did with Jerry and Maria, I had an OBE that proved to me that I was more than my physical body. I was having a sleepless night and tried several relaxation techniques including counting backward and a progressive relaxation technique where I concentrated on relaxing one part of my body at a time. Nothing seemed to work. Then I rolled onto my back and, with my eyes closed, I began to see a vibrating pattern of light. It was kind of like a lattice made out of light. I concentrated on it very intensely, wondering what it was. My hands were folded across my chest, and I could feel vibrations—either my heart thumping rapidly or my whole body vibrating. Then there was a bright flash of light and a snapping sound! I realized my arms and legs were floating up as if I was weightless. But it was February, and I was covered by heavy blankets, so there was no physical way my arms and legs could do that.

> This was not a dream. In fact it was not dreamlike at all!

I had read all of Robert Monroe's books about OBEs by then, so it occurred to me I might be having an OBE. If so, I figured I could rise up, roll over, and look down on my physical body in bed. As I thought those thoughts, I felt the physical sensation of rising into the air. As I rolled over to look down, the rolling sensation was exactly like rolling over physically. This was not a dream. In fact, it was not dreamlike at all!

So I opened my eyes. *Total darkness!* That's all I could see! I was confused, but I still felt myself rising, facing down at this point. Then to my surprise, my face, with my eyes closed, appeared in front of me at close range but moving away. I laughed as I realized I had rolled too soon. I had only risen a few inches, and when I rolled and opened my eyes, they were still inside my head! Guess what? It's really dark in there!

I was fully conscious. I floated up to the ceiling and across the room and could see my physical body lying in bed. I thought about flying across town to visit a friend. She and I had meditated together several times, so I knew she'd be thrilled that I was having an OBE. But then I started to have doubts. It was the middle of the night, and she would probably be asleep. Or she might not be home. And I wasn't sure I wanted to go that far away from my physical body the first time I was out. Suddenly, it was as if these negative thoughts triggered something, and I was flying across the room toward my body, rolling as I went so that I landed on top of my body on my back. My torso immediately reconnected while my arms and legs were loose for a few seconds and then reconnected as well.

> **I now knew beyond any lingering doubts that I was more than my physical body.**

I sat up in bed, totally amazed! I was ecstatic that I had achieved an OBE, but a little disappointed at myself for not controlling it better. I realized that clarity of mind and intent are very important. I could have explored the entire universe, and I didn't get out of my bedroom! But the OBE had a great effect on me. It erased all fear of death. I now knew beyond any lingering doubts that I was more than my physical body.

Although OBEs are outside the scope of this book, I will mention that there are other books available and courses on the subject such as those by

William Buhlman, who teaches a course on OBEs at The Monroe Institute. I have included his information in the bibliography.

There's one more ability you may be able to develop over time, and this one has had a very positive influence on me. It may be a little hard for some of you to swallow, but over the course of several years, I made contact with the souls of six deceased friends and family members and even helped my father move on when he was "stuck" in the afterlife. This is kind of a tricky one because the contact depends not only on you, but on them as well. If they're in a state where they don't want to talk, you're probably not going to find them. They may also be somewhere (a vibrational state) where they're hard to find. I found my grandmother three days after her death. It took a couple of weeks to find my father, and it took over four years to find my mother. I have also contacted deceased friends, but I'm still looking for two close friends after years of trying.

Don't believe that one? Well, I'm certainly not alone in my ability to do this. In fact, The Monroe Institute teaches a couple of courses (one called *Lifelines* and one called *Serving Spirit*) where afterlife contacts are made. *Lifelines*, in particular, has trained hundreds of people to perform "retrievals" of lost souls, to help them move along in the afterlife. I have not taken either of those courses. Maybe if I did, I could find my two lost friends!

Need more proof? How about the experience of a Catholic priest? Father Nathan G. Castle, OP has written a book titled *Afterlife Interrupted: Helping Stuck Souls Cross Over*. Father Nathan has personally contacted and helped over two hundred souls who were temporarily stuck in the afterlife because of the circumstances of their deaths. It's rare for a soul to get stuck, he says, but it does happen. Father Nathan helped them move on.

Your subconscious mind is truly a treasure house within you. What is impressed in the subconscious is expressed in your daily life. When your subconscious mind accepts an idea, any idea, it goes to work to make it come true. This applies equally to negative and positive ideas. If you repeatedly tell yourself, "I'll never have enough money to live comfortably," your subconscious will ensure you remain poor. You will be faced with failure and confusion. On the other hand, if you repeatedly tell yourself, "Large quantities of money easily come to me," your subconscious will ensure you become wealthy. You will have guidance and peace of mind.

The key, then, is to avoid negative thoughts. But how do you do that? If you were in desperate need of more money you might say a simple prayer, "I need more money" or "I want more money." But in your mind, you would also be thinking, "But I can't get it. I have no skills for earning lots of money." You have two contradictory ideas and your subconscious always accepts the dominant idea. That's why you often get the opposite of what you ask for. You voiced a desire, but then imagined roadblocks that would prevent you from getting it. Your imagined negative thoughts neutralized your desire. What you need is a methodology that reconciles the conflict between desire and imagination.

Here's a method for doing that. First, you want to enter into a drowsy, sleepy state. The best time to do this is just before going to sleep in the evening or just after you awaken in the morning. In this state, the negative thoughts that were neutralizing your desire are suppressed. Second, imagine the reality of your fulfilled desire and feel the thrill of your new circumstances. For example, you may want to meet the perfect romantic partner. Just imagine that you have done so and feel how happy you are. Don't try to force it. Don't make a lot of effort. Just relax and enjoy knowing that your subconscious mind is at work fulfilling your desire.

Does this work instantly? No. But repeat the process daily for several weeks and watch miracles happen. Learn to use your subconscious mind constructively and you will be healthier, wealthier, wiser, and happier. You can use your subconscious to overcome health problems, wealth problems, marital problems, and interpersonal relationship problems as well. The list goes on and on.

I used to believe that *if* the abilities I noted above were true, they were reserved for a few people who were natural-born psychics or mediums. Now that I, a science-oriented skeptic, have learned to demonstrate those abilities, I believe that *anyone* can learn to do them. Learn the techniques and *practice*. Like anything else, if you want to do it well, you have to practice. It's like the old joke where the tourist in New York City, seeking directions, asks the musician, "How do you get to Carnegie Hall?"

"Practice, practice, practice."

CHAPTER 4

Negative, Limiting Beliefs Can Hold You Back

Various mental states and beliefs might be holding you back from experiencing psychic functioning or having profound spiritual experiences. I want to help you change those mental states and beliefs so that you'll be wildly successful in your experiments and your further exploration of expanded consciousness. In short, change your beliefs—change your life.

Maybe you're open to the idea, but are afraid of what other people will think of you if you tell them you believe in psychic functioning or that you have had a profound spiritual experience. Will they think less of you? Will they shun you? Will they think you're nuts?

To that, I ask, *Really? You would give up all the benefits we discussed in the previous chapter because you're afraid of what other people will think of you?*

> It's your life! Experiment. Find out
> what you're fully capable of.

Don't let what other people think of you limit your development as a human being. It's *your* life! Experiment. Find out what you're fully capable of. If you don't want to tell other people, then don't tell them. You can learn to use your subconscious mind to do amazing things and keep those abilities to yourself if you want. At least you would have a greater appreciation for the mystery of life we're all involved in.

I decided to tell other people about the amazing things that were happening to me, and it's one of the greatest decisions I ever made. Why? Because it *confirmed* things for me. The vast majority of people I told didn't condemn me. They didn't think I was nuts. In fact, they confided that they, or someone close to them, had had similar experiences! And that confirmation really boosted my confidence that what I was discovering was *real*. In all likelihood, you'll find the same thing is true with the people you tell.

Let me tell you some surprising reactions I observed. When I did my successful ESP experiment with Jerry and Maria, I was working as an outside independent patent attorney doing work for a major corporation. I decided to tell several of the engineers and attorneys working in my client's patent department about the experiment. I knew there was the potential they would think I had gone crazy and would stop sending me work, but I planned to prevent that by presenting the results and then asking their opinion. I showed them the drawings and explained how we had taken great care to make sure no hints were given during the sessions, and then I asked, "What do you think about that? Does it surprise you?"

Most of them weren't surprised at all. Their response was to tell me about their own psychic or spiritual experiences! I couldn't believe it. These professional, science-oriented engineers started me telling about their experiences with telepathy, energy work, psychic healing, past-life regression, and visitations by deceased relatives!

One engineer told me that back before the days of cell phones, her mother used telepathy to send messages to her father. She recalled how one time her father had gone to the grocery store and her mother was frustrated because she had forgotten to tell him to get a bottle brush—one of those skinny brushes you can stick down the narrow neck of a bottle to clean the inside. She said her mother sat down at the kitchen table for a couple of minutes and rested her head in her hands. She then got up and said, "There!" and went about her business. When her father returned and was unpacking the groceries, he pulled a bottle brush out of the bag and said, "I thought we might need one of these." Isn't that amazing?

This same engineer told me she psychically cured herself of appendicitis (psychic healing is usually classified as a form of psychokinesis, i.e., affecting matter with the mind, rather than ESP). She had been admitted to the hospital after medical tests definitively showed appendicitis. Surgery was scheduled for the next morning. That night, as she lay in the hospital bed, she repeatedly envisioned a sphere of energy surrounding her appendix and then floating away—carrying the infection out of her body. When the doctors examined her the next morning, they were amazed. She was perfectly fine! There was no sign of infection. The appendix was healthy, and the hospital released her.

Another engineer told me he could see people's auras—energy fields of different colors emanating from their bodies.

Other examples happened recently after I published my novel, *An Adventurous Soul*. As I mentioned earlier, it's about one soul's exciting journey through what I call the "Human Learning School." The soul, Barbara, decides she wants to try the School and lives multiple human lives.

A patent agent who I had worked with for many years read the book and sent me an amazing email. He works in a highly technical field, so I wasn't sure how he would respond. Imagine my surprise when he told me he knew he had lived before, and remembered how he had died in a prior life! Here's what he wrote:

> I have always taken the position that I do not need to know about life energy beyond our four dimensions because I was here to enjoy the present life. I know I have had other lives. This present life is one in which [my wife] and I were destined to live out our true love—it having been prevented in a previous life when her father and her brother threw me over a cliff into the sea.... I feel it happened in Spain in the dark ages and the sea was the Atlantic. I fell 200 feet or so into the water—I can still see the water coming at me as I fell. It was at night, the moon was bright, and the weather was windy with large waves crashing into the foot of the cliff. I was a good swimmer, but to no avail, I died on impact with the water.

He also said my book had gotten him thinking about exploring his spirituality. He said, "Throughout my life I have meditated. After reading your book, I am going to see if I can make it a daily practice again with a view to connecting with those in Level four, so to speak."

Level four, by the way, is a reference to a very high spiritual level that's part of the story in *An Adventurous Soul*. Souls at that level are last-timers—those preparing for their final human experience before reuniting with God. When they return to human form, most of them lead quiet lives, staying out of the limelight, but showing great love, compassion, and forgiveness toward their fellow humans. A few, however, become great spiritual Speakers in their final lifetime and teach about mankind's true nature.

Another example of a surprising reaction to my ESP and spiritual experiences involves a husband and wife I worked with during my years as a radar engineer at GE. The husband was an engineer and project manager, and the wife was a proposal specialist who worked on a team that put together offers to the government on major defense programs. Today, she works as a well-known business coach. The husband, whose mother passed away several years ago, called me after reading *An Adventurous Soul* and told me that as he and his wife do things around the house, she often stops and tells him, "Your mother's here again." Apparently, she can sense her mother-in-law's presence—something most of us would dread! Neither of them had ever mentioned anything like that to me before.

So, you never know. Your fears of what people will think of you may be totally misplaced.

Maybe you're being held back by the belief that subconscious communication—that is, psychic and spiritual experiences—are against your religion. I don't know of any religion, however, that precludes you from living a fulfilled life of high quality. In fact, most religions teach that God/the higher power wants us to live fulfilled and high-quality lives. The benefits of discovering your subconscious powers, which I described in Chapter 3, do just that. Let's look briefly at those benefits in light of religious teachings.

Empowerment gives us the feeling of being in control of our lives rather than being victims of circumstances beyond our control. King Solomon and the teachings of the book of Proverbs would certainly support the fact that we should strive for empowerment. Receiving signs and experiencing serendipitous events could be construed as being led by the Holy Spirit. Querying the universe to learn the nature of our existence is like asking God for answers. Improved intuition could be seen as God providing answers to us as we go through our daily lives.

Some people may have problems with other benefits, such as the ability to remote view, having out-of-body experiences (OBEs), and contacting souls in the afterlife. But I know of no religious texts that prohibit these activities. Remote viewing wasn't even identified as a human capability until very recently. So there is nothing in any religious text that says don't do it. There have been reports of people having OBEs throughout history, including prophets and saints. In ancient Egypt, the Egyptian priests called the astral body the Kha. There are inscriptions and drawings on the rock walls of many temples and buildings, representing the Kha as something subtle and light abandoning the physical body. In the Bible, the book of Revelation, Chapter 4 gives a complete description of an OBE experienced by the author, John.

Religious texts that say getting to heaven is a matter of having faith are, in my opinion, directed toward people who have not experienced their spiritual nature firsthand. No religious text says we have to wait until we die to receive confirmation that we are spiritual beings.

As far as afterlife contact is concerned, I mentioned that the Catholic priest, Father Nathan Castle, has contacted and helped over two hundred souls in the afterlife. His religious superior confirmed that Father Nathan's work is in faithfulness to the Church.

Note also that St. Paul recognized that people can have prophetic (i.e., psychic) powers. He cautioned people not to use those powers arrogantly, but to use them with love. In his first letter to the Corinthians, Chapter 13:2, St. Paul says, "And if I have prophetic powers, and understand all mysteries and all knowledge, and if I have all faith so as to remove mountains, but have not love, I am nothing."

Another belief that can hold you back is believing that physical matter is all there is. If that's what you believe, you may think psychic and spiritual experiences are caused by some misfiring neurons in the brain. I used to think that. To me, the universe consisted of what I could perceive with my five physical senses. I believed that people invented religions over the years because they were afraid of death.

If that's you as well, you may argue that conventional scientists don't believe psychic and spiritual experiences are real, so why should you? Science has progressed pretty far in the last two to three hundred years, and you think they have it right.

But the question is, have they *ever* had it right?

Steven Ware Smith

> Remember, science advances funeral by funeral.

At every point in time, scientists were sure their theory of the universe was correct. Change came only with great effort—and *time*. More often than not, new ideas were rejected by the established experts, who tended to cling desperately to their old model. It wasn't until a new generation came along, a generation who grew up thinking about a new idea, that it was studied and eventually accepted. As the saying goes (attributed variously to a dozen famous scientists), "Science advances funeral by funeral."

Until a few hundred years ago, any scientist would tell you the Earth was flat and it was the only planet in the universe. To them, the other planets in our solar system were mere dots of light. They were wandering stars. Everything circled the Earth. We were the center of the universe. This was intuitively obvious—you could just look up and see it for yourself.

But Aristarchus of Samos, a Greek mathematician and astronomer, first proposed that the sun is the center of the solar system about 2400 years ago. His idea obviously didn't get much traction with the scientists of the day or for many centuries thereafter. The first *modern* astronomer to propose a sun-centered solar system was Nikolai Copernicus in 1535. It didn't catch on quickly that time, either. About 80 years later, Galileo Galilei was the first to use a telescope for astronomy and discovered that the wandering stars were planets, not points of light like the stars. He saw mountains and craters on the moon and discovered that it's a whole other world. He saw four moons (Ganymede, Io, Europa, and Callisto) circling Jupiter—the first objects found to orbit a body other than Earth or the sun. What was his reward for these great discoveries? He was condemned for writing about his discoveries and was sentenced to house arrest for the rest of his life!

When Albert Einstein published his paper on special relativity in 1905, the reception wasn't exactly warm either. Einstein argued that space and time were bound up together, a complicated idea that contradicted the long-held belief in something called "ether." Scientists of the time believed that everything that moved as a wave had to have a substance that supported its movement. For example, sound had to have air to move through. Waves in the ocean needed water. Light, they figured, needed an invisible substance called ether to support its travel through space. Einstein's theory noted there was no experimental confirmation for the substance. There was no proof it existed, other than that the scientific establishment had accepted the concept.

> Scientists have always had it wrong, but always thought they were right. Isn't it rather foolish, and arrogant, to think they have it correct now?

For years after Einstein put his contradiction of ether out into the world, no one took it seriously except the scientists in his home country of Germany. The idea of ether had originated in Britain, and there Einstein's idea fell on totally deaf ears. His theory was complicated, and many scientists didn't understand it. A few understood it in the U.S., but generally considered it impractical and absurd. It took many years of examination, criticism, and elaboration before relativity was accepted.

So in essence, scientists have always had it wrong, but have always thought they were correct. Isn't it rather foolish and arrogant to think they have it correct now?

But maybe you hesitate to discard our current scientific model. After all, it does a pretty good job of explaining most of the workings of our physical universe, as long as you don't look at things that are too big, too fast, or too small. But it doesn't explain psychic phenomena such as remote viewing, where viewers have repeatedly demonstrated, under very strictly controlled conditions, the ability to gather accurate, detailed information on people, places, and events well beyond the range of their physical senses in both space and time.

But just because our current scientific model doesn't explain *everything*, it doesn't mean we have to discard the current model entirely—and I'm not suggesting that you do. The model just needs to be expanded to include processes we don't currently understand. It could merely be that, like it has been throughout history, our understanding of the world is simply incomplete.

If you're a scientist, it's foolish to think we know it all. Dark matter? Dark energy? What the heck are those? At best, they're just constructs we're using to try to explain astronomical measurements that don't match what we expected to see. They're our best guess, but we don't know if they exist. Perhaps time passes at different rates in different parts of the universe. That would explain a lot of the weirdness we see out there.

Maybe you're not a scientist but believe conventional scientists when they say ESP is impossible. But where would we be today if, throughout history, everyone had listened when others said, "That can't be done"?

> Let's do what real scientists should do, and explore the unknown!

As a scientist, the results obtained in controlled psychic experiments excite me. The results are undeniably positive, but we don't know the mechanism. It's the new frontier, and studying it, instead of ridiculing it or fearing it, seems to be the sensible thing to do, given the overwhelming evidence that it's real. Accepting the reality of psychic functioning will not destroy science as we know it. It won't push us back into the Dark Ages, where superstition and magical thinking take over. Instead, it will propel us into a new era in which we begin to understand the very nature of our existence as sentient beings.

Consciousness is the basis of how we experience life, yet we have no idea what consciousness is or how it's created. Let's do what real scientists should do, and explore the unknown!

CHAPTER 5

If You Think ESP Is Strange, Take A Look At Modern Physics

So you think ESP is strange, and you believe conventional physicists when they say ESP is impossible. Well guess what? If you believe what those guys say, you believe in some pretty strange stuff already. The weirdness of modern physics is just as strange as or stranger than ESP. Let's take a look.

At a very large scale, there's the Theory of Relativity. Relativity tells us that any object with mass warps space-time around it, meaning it actually warps empty space and changes how fast time passes. *Okay...*

Or how about this one: time slows down more and more the faster you move. Physicists call this "time dilation." Some pretty strange things result from time dilation. For example, the physics equations governing time dilation show that if you were in a spaceship traveling near the speed of light, your time would essentially stop. You could travel anywhere in the universe and it would seem to you, on your spaceship, that you got there almost instantly. But time would pass more quickly for those of us back here on Earth because we're not moving anywhere near that fast.

In a way, this enables you to time-travel to the future. As you may know, a light-year is defined as the distance that light travels in one year while moving at the rate of 186,000 miles per second. Now let's assume you're in that really fast spaceship, and you travel near the speed of light from Earth to another planet fifty light-years away. Because of time dilation, you would experience that you got there almost instantly. If you then turned around and returned fifty light-years to Earth at the same speed, it would seem to you that you got back almost instantly. So for this round trip, almost no time would have gone by for you, on the spaceship, but it would be one hundred years later on Earth. All your friends and immediate family would be long dead, but you could say hello to your great-great-great grandkids!

> **Even things that sound really weird can be true.**

I'm not making this stuff up. It seems weird, but we have evidence that time dilation is real. Satellites in low orbit around the Earth travel about 17,000 miles per hour. That's nowhere near the speed of light, but it's fast enough to see some effects of time dilation. Most notably, it can be seen in the very precise timing signals that are sent to and from Global Positioning System (GPS) satellites in orbit. Corrections have to be made to the timing signals to counteract the time-dilation effects. If those corrections weren't made, GPS locations would be much less accurate.

So even things that sound weird (like ESP—hint, hint!) can be true.

Here's another mind-bender about the so-called laws of physics. The equations governing many of the laws of physics are time-reversible. This means we could, for example, film a physical system in motion, and then play the film backward to see what happens. If the backward film displays a motion that is always possible, the system is said to be time-reversal invariant. Otherwise, it is not.

Our solar system is an example of a system that is time-reversal invariant. If we look "down" on the solar system from an imaginary spaceship high above the northern hemisphere of Earth (of course, there's not really an up or down in space, but let's stick with the convention that north is up and south is down), the planets would appear to be orbiting the sun in a counter-clockwise direction. If time ran backward, the planets would reverse course and orbit in a clockwise direction. Is this possible? Of course it is! In fact, the direction of the planets' orbits depends entirely on your perspective. If we were to fly our spaceship to a point far below the southern hemisphere of Earth, so that we are looking "up" at the solar system, the planets would appear to be orbiting the sun in a clockwise direction. If you're having trouble visualizing this, put a marble in a clear glass jar and get the marble rolling around the bottom in a counter-clockwise direction as you look down at it. Now raise the jar and observe the marble from below. It will be moving clockwise from your new perspective.

So massive objects, like planets, can appear to move in the reverse direction if time is reversed. As a result, some scientists contend that "time reversal" is a misnomer; it is really "direction reversal." But what happens when we look at things at the quantum level? After all, in quantum mechanics, a time reversal operator Θ acting on a state produces a state that evolves backward in time. With multiple quantum particles in a system, what happens to their position, their momentum, and their spin when the time reversal operator comes into play? There's no agreement among scientists, and since we never see time running backward, we just discard the mathematical solutions that indicate backward time. Is that the right thing to do? Maybe those solutions hold the key to faster-than-light travel, or time travel, or anti-gravity machines, or teleportation. (Beam me up, Scotty!) Who knows? We just throw out those solutions as being nonsense, because we've never seen time running backward. But if it does, and it's beyond our conscious perception, there could be immense implications.

Our attitude toward those backward time solutions reminds me of the story about European explorers coming ashore in the Americas and meeting Native Americans. The story goes that when the Europeans explained they came in that "boat" anchored offshore, the Native Americans were not able to see it. The sailing ship of the Europeans was so vastly different from what the Native Americans considered to be a boat, they looked right past the large sailing ship looking for something more like a canoe.

I don't know whether that story is true or not, but it highlights a basic human tendency to recognize that with which we are familiar as being true or real and that with which we are not familiar as being false or nonexistent.

Finally, keep this in mind: the theory of relativity requires that nothing, not even *information*, can travel faster than light. If you thought relativity was weird, welcome to the weird world of *quantum mechanics*—the theory of the very small.

The theory of quantum mechanics says that before subatomic quantum particles such as electrons or photons are measured, they are only a probabilistic wave function. A probabilistic wave function in quantum physics is a complex mathematical equation describing the quantum state of a quantum particle. The wave function can be used to predict values of possible measurements that can be made for the particle, such as its location, velocity, or spin.

You can think of the wave function as a superposition, that is, an overlap of all the different locations the particle could possibly be in. It may be more likely that the particle is in one location than another, but before you look at the particle, it's not in *any* definite location. But when you look at it, that is, detect it or measure it, the wave function is said to "collapse" and the location becomes known. It's really weird to think that the behavior of this object is different depending on whether you're looking at it or not. That's the fundamental weirdness of quantum mechanics: that objects behave one way when you're not looking at them, and in another way when you are. Strange.

A famous experiment in quantum mechanics, known as the "double-slit experiment," demonstrates this "observer effect." The experiment shows that subatomic particles (and even some atoms and molecules) behave as energy waves when not observed, and behave as particles when observed.

In this experiment, a beam of electrons is fired at two parallel slits in a first flat plate. Each electron goes through one or the other of the slits and hits a second flat plate on the other side. If it's unknown which slit each electron goes through, the electrons behave like energy waves. So when they go through the slits, they spread out on the backside like ripples in a pond when you throw in a stone. The waves interfere with each other on the backside of the slits and form an interference pattern on the second flat plate. It looks something like this:

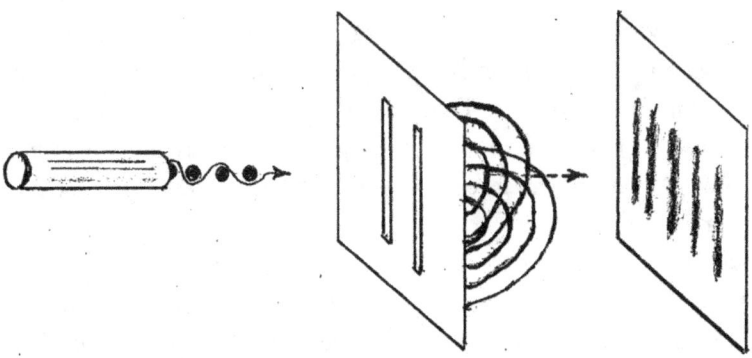

But if you put a detector at one of the slits so that you then know which slit each electron goes through, the electrons change their behavior. They behave instead like discrete physical particles. Instead of the interference pattern, they form only a single line behind each slit showing they went through the slits like little BBs instead of waves.

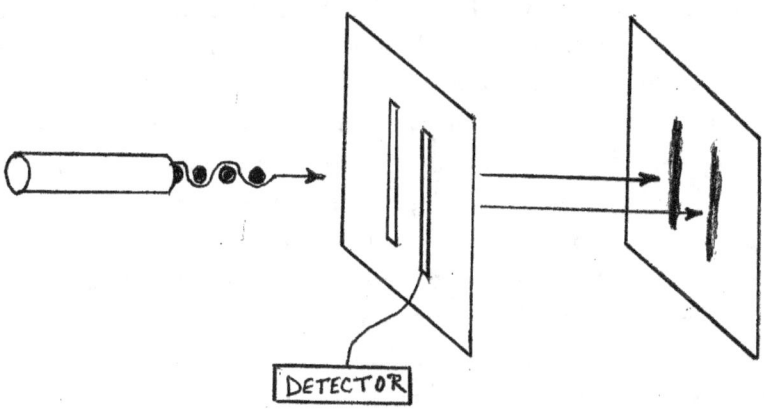

That's right—simply having knowledge of which slit the electrons go through causes quantum particles to behave differently. Hmm… things are getting weird!

Oh, and by the way, when you're not using the detector, you can fire the electrons one at a time and still get the interference pattern. Weirder still. What are they interfering with if they go through one at a time?

Quantum entanglement is another weird aspect of quantum mechanics. If a high-energy quantum particle having certain properties is split into two lower-energy particles, each of the split particles will have properties that are complementary to each other. That is, if their properties are added together, they equal the properties of the original high-energy particle. However, in the usual quantum fashion, we can't know which properties each particle has until it is measured.

Now here's the weird part. No matter how far apart those two particles travel, they are still linked together or *entangled*, somehow. As soon as a measurement of one of the split particles is made, the other split particle instantly displays the complementary properties. *Instantly*. It would seem the information about the measurement is transmitted *instantaneously* between the particles, thus violating the speed of light limitation of the theory of relativity. This has been verified in experiments measuring entangled particles separated by many miles. Theoretically, they could be light-years apart and the information would be instantly conveyed. Hmm... things are getting weirder!

Okay, one last thing before we leave this physics stuff behind (at least until Chapter 12, where I'll put forth some theories about how psychic functioning works). The physicist Max Planck discovered there are minimum units of distance and time in our universe. Two objects cannot be less than a Planck length apart, and two events cannot be separated in time by less than a Planck time. The Planck length is extremely tiny (roughly equal to 1.6×10^{-35} meters). That's 1.6 meters divided by 1 with 35 zeros after it. The Planck time is the time it would take a photon traveling at the speed of light to cross a distance equal to the Planck length. That's roughly equal to 10^{-43} seconds or 1 divided by 1 with 43 zeros after it. As I said, those are *really* small numbers, but what the Planck length and the Planck time actually tell us is that at the very smallest scale, the physical universe is laid out in an array of these tiny little space/time *pixels*. On the smallest scale, the physical universe is *digital*! Are you still believing what conventional scientists say is true?

Hmm... maybe we're living in a virtual reality. Maybe this is all just a computer simulation, and sensory inputs are being generated and fed to our brains by a giant computer in the sky. Actually, it would be a nice, tidy explanation for quantum entanglement. Those entangled particles that instantly transmitted information between them weren't really miles or light-years apart—they're just simulations on the same hard drive. So in a virtual reality, quantum entanglement doesn't violate the speed-of-light limitation after all!

Well, I'm not proposing we're in a virtual reality, but it's something interesting to think about. However, there is at least one nuclear physicist who thinks it's true. His name is Tom Campbell, and he has a lot of YouTube videos where he describes his "Big TOE," where TOE stands for Theory Of Everything. He also teaches a course (*My Big TOE*) at The Monroe Institute. Check it out if you want to learn a little more about whether we're living in a virtual reality—but you better sign up early, because this intensive program is only offered once every two years, and it fills quickly.

In any event, the bottom line on physics is that hundreds of experiments have verified the theory of relativity for the very large and fast-moving, and hundreds of experiments have verified quantum mechanics for the very small. However, the two theories are incompatible. One prohibits information from traveling faster than light, and the other demonstrates that it does. Yet scientists believe in both of them. Does that make sense?

Meanwhile, hundreds of tightly controlled experiments have verified that psychic functioning is real. So why hasn't it been accepted by conventional scientists, when they readily accept stuff just as weird and even contradictory?

One contributing factor could be the human characteristic referred to as "directed reasoning" or "confirmation bias." *We all do this.* If a person has strong emotions about a belief, they will solidify that belief by picking and choosing bits of information that support the belief, while ignoring information that refutes it. Most of us believe we have open minds and are ready to change our opinions as we take in new information, but in reality, we seek out and embrace information that confirms our preexisting beliefs and ignore the rest, rather than weigh each piece of evidence equally. No amount of logic or facts will convince someone affected by confirmation bias to change his or her mind. It's like arguing with a brick wall.

Surprisingly, highly educated people (like scientists) are more likely to fall prey to confirmation bias than less educated people. This is probably because the highly educated have a broader field of knowledge from which to draw pseudo-evidence to support their beliefs.

Think about it, and do some self-analysis. I had to do that after the 1996 ESP experiment shattered the materialist worldview I was deeply reliant upon—and it was excruciatingly painful! Are you determined, for some reason, to hold onto your existing worldview that says psychic functioning is impossible? If so, try to figure out why you're holding onto that belief. Maybe you feel threatened by psychic phenomena—for example, it may bother you to think that the thoughts that pop into your head may not be solely your own. If that bothers you, you are probably going to hold onto your pre-existing beliefs for dear life. Nothing will convince you. You're an island. You're a brick wall.

Another factor contributing to the rejection of psychic functioning by many scientists is that it seems the results of psychic experiments are not consistently repeatable. Even the very best remote viewers in the world have "misses" where their description of the assigned target is completely wrong. Also, viewers are not 100 percent accurate even when they are "on target." An overall score of 85-90 percent correct is fantastic! Some viewers are that good or better at sensing *some* aspect of the target such as its color, but they're not so accurate with some other aspect, like the shape. Others are extremely accurate at describing people, but if the target is a piece of electronic equipment, their accuracy is no better than "chance," that is, the probability of correctly *guessing* the viewed information!

This inconsistency is a *huge* problem for conventional scientists. They believe that when you run an experiment under the same conditions multiple times, you should get the exact same result every time. The physical world has to be consistent. When you drop a tennis ball, it should fall to the ground every time. It shouldn't stay suspended in mid-air sometimes, or go up other times! When you mix chemicals in a beaker in a chemistry lab multiple times under the same conditions, the chemical reaction should be the same every time. You shouldn't have to wonder, "What's it going to do this time? Blow up, or turn purple?"

At the quantum level, as weird as the double-slit experiment and the entangled particle experiment are, they're consistent. You get the same weird result each time you run them.

The seemingly inconsistent results of psychic functioning cause skeptics to say, "See, it doesn't work!" However, I believe remote viewing experiments *can be* consistent, but the results appear mixed for at least three reasons. First, the intent of all the participants has to be aligned. *Intent* drives everything. That means the tasker, the administrator, the monitor, the viewer, and the judge who determines the correctness of the viewed information all have to agree on what they intend to accomplish in the remote viewing session. Otherwise, you are likely to get a bad result.

For example, a police department may contact a remote viewing company and tell an administrator there that they need a description of the house where a hostage is being held. The administrator may think this is not good tasking for the viewer because it assumes the hostage is in a house when he may not be. Additionally, houses in the area all look very similar, so even an accurate description will not help much. So the administrator decides it would be better to task the viewer with identifying prominent landmarks near the hostage and providing the direction and distance of each landmark from the hostage. If the tasker and the administrator don't come to an agreement and align their intent, the outcome is likely to be poor.

The second reason that remote-viewing results appear mixed is what I call a mistranslation between the subconscious mind and the conscious mind of the viewer. I believe the subconscious mind receives accurate information about the target and presents it to the conscious mind symbolically. When the conscious mind doesn't recognize a symbol, it makes something up. This made-up information may or may not have anything to do with the target. By doing dozens or hundreds of practice remote-viewing sessions, the viewer comes to know the symbolic language of his/her subconscious mind. Translation accuracy then becomes very high.

The third reason for remote-viewing results to appear mixed is broadly classified as mental noise. Mental noise is an overlay of memories, conjectures, inferences, pattern-fitting, speculation, conclusion-jumping, and so on that tends to compete with the comparatively quiet and fleeting ESP signal from the subconscious mind.

In particular, the viewers' conscious minds interfere in the process and try to guess the target without enough information. The problem is that viewers can't always recognize when their conscious minds have intervened. So they get off track when their conscious mind guesses wrong. I'll discuss this in more detail in Chapters 10 and 11 on Controlled Remote Viewing.

As a result of these inconsistencies, most remote viewing studies report the results as a statistical deviation from "chance." They look at the percentage of target characteristics the viewer correctly described, and calculate the probability of correctly guessing that percentage. But as we all know, statistics can be manipulated to show just about anything the author wants to say—for instance, in a photo of horses being led back to a barn by their riders, a statistician could say the average animal in the photo has three legs! So conventional scientists don't think using statistics is good enough.

However, some of the results of psychic experiments reported by physicists at Stanford Research Institute in the 1970s were beyond reproach. In one such experiment, the viewer, Hella Hammid, remote-viewed nine distantly located targets with such accuracy that the odds were calculated as less than two in a million (1.8×10^{-6}) that Hella could have done what she did by chance. After SRI published the results, the experiment was successfully replicated at Princeton University and universities in Russia, Holland, and Scotland. By 1982, fifteen successful replications had been performed. Details are described in chapter four of Russell Targ's book, *The Reality of ESP: A Physicist's Proof of Psychic Abilities*.

When it is *repeatedly* shown that remote viewing results can be this accurate, you have to recognize that something unknown is happening. Ignoring it or turning a blind eye is simply ridiculous.

When it comes right down to it, believing that psychic phenomena are real is no stranger than believing in relativity and quantum mechanics. The strangeness of the universe we live in seems to have no limits, either at the very large scale (relativity) or the very small scale (quantum mechanics). So why put limits on psychic functioning, which has solid scientific evidence?

A funny story about putting limits on the universe is found in Edwin Abbott's 1884 novel called, *Flatland: A Romance of Many Dimensions*. Abbott describes a 2-dimensional society where the inhabitants live on a flat surface, and all the inhabitants are flat, too. Different types of inhabitants are distinguished from others by being different geometric shapes—like circles, triangles, and squares. They can only move in two dimensions—forward and backward, and right and left. There is no up and down. The inhabitants there are completely unaware of that third dimension—height. In the story, one of them has a mystical experience where he rises above their plane of existence and looks down on their realm. He becomes aware of height. But when he tries to teach about it, he's imprisoned! "He's crazy!" everyone says. "There's no other dimension. Lock him up!"

Another story I like about understanding the universe is a story about a marksman who shoots a series of holes every five inches across the surface of a target. A society of 2-dimensional entities evolves on the surface of the target and begin to study their flat, 2-dimensional universe. Finally, after years of study and discussion, their scientists figure it out. They gather everyone together and proclaim that the nature of the universe is that there is a hole in the universe every five inches.

Think about that one! Put yourself in their position and see if you could draw a different conclusion. If your perspective is limited to two dimensions, probably not!

So what's the common factor in these two stories? Why did I tell them to you? Both *Flatland* and the target story have characters who make determinations about the nature of the universe based on *too little information.* Don't do that!

Try to envision being enclosed in a bubble. In essence, we all walk around in what I call a "perception bubble." It surrounds us and feeds us information through all of our five physical senses. Our perception bubble defines our universe because it provides us all the information we get.

Suppose, in reality, you exist as a brain in a jar on a laboratory shelf. Five electrodes are attached to your brain, each supplying the brain with sensory inputs mocking one of the five physical senses. You sense that you are outdoors standing on a sidewalk looking down a tree-lined street with houses. You feel the wind blowing on your face and hair. It's a pleasant temperature and the sky is mostly clear with a few puffy white clouds. You hear children playing and smell bread baking in someone's home. You can see as far as some trees on a distant ridge that rises and blocks your view of anything beyond. Is this real? What's beyond the hill? Anything? You don't know so you walk in that direction. As you do, a new scene unfolds before you. Eventually, you walk over the top of the ridge and a little way down the far side and see a new scene stretching out before you. You turn around and look back in the direction that you came, and you can no longer see where you started. Is it still there? You assume it is, but is it?

These may seem like silly questions, but in reality, there's no way for you to know. In this example, your perception bubble, like most people's, is defined by what you can perceive with your five physical senses. That's your universe.

But what if you're like a Flatlander? What if there's another dimension that some people claim they have experienced, and you haven't? A dimension that's real. A dimension that can reveal to you that your perception of reality is incomplete. A dimension people refer to as psychic, spiritual, or mystical because they have no better name for it.

Personally, I don't want to be close-minded like the Flatlanders or misinformed about the nature of reality like the target people—especially when there is solid scientific evidence and *millions* of people saying they have experienced this other dimension.

> **Several types of ESP experiments appear to violate the causal closure principle of physicalism.**

If you're a die-hard physicalist you may still not be convinced. To convince a physicalist that ESP is real, I would have to demonstrate that ESP violates some basic principle of physicalism. A principle that comes to mind is causal closure. This principle essentially says that the physical universe is a closed system. Any event that happens in the physical universe has to have been caused by another, previous event in the physical universe. Thus, nothing from outside the physical universe can initiate or interrupt a causal chain of events. Several types of ESP experiments, however, provide evidence that they violate the causal closure principle.

First, experiments referred to as "presentiment experiments" show that human subjects can experience an autonomic response to an emotionally charged stimulus several seconds in advance of being presented with the stimulus. For example, a subject's eyes may dilate and her heart rate may increase before she is shown a gruesome photograph of an accident scene. These experiments appear to violate causal closure through precognition (i.e., becoming aware of a future event). In these experiments, there is no previous event in the physical universe that causes the autonomic response.

Second, remote viewing experiments show that human subjects, when sequestered from all known means of communication, can perceive and accurately describe remote physical locations, objects, people, and events. These experiments appear to violate causal closure through remote awareness and non-physically mediated perception-at-a-distance. In these experiments, there is no event in the physical universe that transports the perceived information to the viewer before the viewer provides the description.

Third, Associative Remote Viewing (ARV) experiments show that human subjects can describe a target that will not be presented to them until sometime in the future. The target is usually associated with the outcome of a future binary event such as a sporting event. These experiments appear to violate closure through both remote awareness and precognition.

In a typical remote viewing session, a tasker decides what target will be viewed. The tasker assigns a reference number to the target and then provides only the reference number to the viewer and to a person serving as a monitor if a monitor is being used. The viewer's mind must then do two things that appear to violate causal closure. First, the viewer's mind must associate the reference number with the target without any known physical communication whatsoever. Second, the viewer's mind must then access descriptive information about the target, again without any known physical communication whatsoever. This seemingly miraculous process is being performed daily by hundreds of trained remote viewers and students.

So with all the evidence for ESP piling up, what's preventing you from experiencing psychic functioning? In all probability, your quest for expanded consciousness is being bogged down by negative limiting beliefs. Hopefully, the preceding discussion has shown you that beliefs about people's negative reactions and beliefs about science should not prevent you from experiencing psychic functioning. But you may have other negative beliefs still holding you hostage. So how can you get rid of those rascals? That's what we're going to study next.

CHAPTER 6

Get Your Mind Right!

Let's talk a little about limiting beliefs: those nagging doubts about yourself or your abilities that you have carried around for as long as you can remember (and beyond). When we let those thoughts control us—when we succumb to fear, despair, or overwhelm—some people say we're "dancing with the Devil." And the Devil is leading the dance. So how can we identify those devilish thoughts and get rid of them? How can we retake the lead in the dance of life?

Many years ago there was a TV show called "The $64,000 Question." That title came to symbolize any question that seemed impossible, or at least very difficult, to answer. That's what we have here—a $64,000 question. Identifying limiting beliefs is difficult. We've carried them around for so long, they're just part of our identity. How do you identify and eliminate something that's an integral part of you?

We're conscious of some of these limiting beliefs, even if we don't actively think about them as we go through our daily activities. They take the form of things we "just know" we're not good at. These aren't random thoughts; we have accumulated good evidence over the years that we're really not good at these things. So they don't seem like beliefs—they seem like *facts*.

For example, when I was very young I wanted to be an artist. But my drawings were very mechanical and, frankly, not very good. So I formed the belief that I'm not artistic. Over the years, I have seen time after time that I just can't draw very well. To cover my disappointment, I have always joked that I'm not the "artsy-fartsy" type. I convinced myself that my strengths lie elsewhere.

Here's another example. When I was about five or six years old, my mother signed me up for piano lessons. I liked playing and decided I wanted to become a musician, but my playing, like my drawing, was very mechanical, and I didn't seem to have an "ear" for music. It took me quite a while to learn to play "Mary Had a Little Lamb," plunking the keys one note at a time. I formed the belief that I'm just not musically inclined. Again, I covered my disappointment by joking about it. I told people I couldn't carry a tune in a bucket.

Have you known for practically all your life that you're not good at certain skills? Have you had lots of experiences that have proven your weaknesses? Do you have areas of your life where you joke about your inadequacies? Have you never had a psychic or spiritual experience? If you answered yes to any of these questions, those may be good places to start your search for limiting beliefs.

Since I was aware of my limiting beliefs regarding art and music, I was able to address them head-on. When I was a teenager, I took some guitar lessons and, after a *lot* of practice, became good enough to impress my father with my ability to play classical guitar music. I could even do it without looking at the music. I did well enough to convince myself I wasn't so musically inept after all.

Recently, I addressed my belief that I was not artistic. At the time, I was still a stick-figure type of artist—really pathetic! So I bought the book, *Drawing on the Right Side of the Brain*, by Betty Edwards. As I read about Betty's techniques for teaching people how to draw, I realized my subconscious mind had been causing me to draw poorly because my failures reinforced my negative belief that I was not artistic.

In Betty's classes, she has her students draw a picture of their hand before receiving any instruction. Then they learn and practice some of her techniques and draw their hand again. Here's a drawing I did of my hand before practicing Betty's techniques:

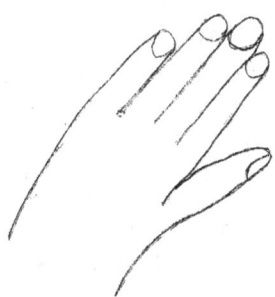

By paying attention to details and practicing Betty's techniques, my drawing ability improved dramatically. Here's a drawing I did of my hand just a few days later:

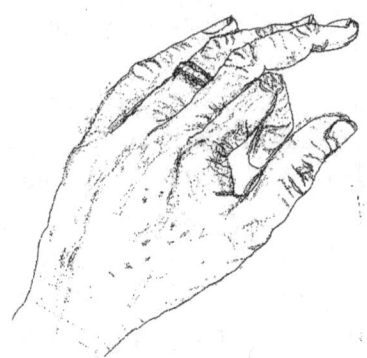

Hey, I'm still no Michelangelo, but I impressed *myself*, and that's what matters when you're overcoming a limiting belief.

It's often said that skills such as musical ability and artistic ability are widely distributed in the population, and everyone has some ability and can participate to some extent. Even the most non-musical person can learn to play a tune on the piano, and even the most artistically-challenged person can learn to draw reasonably well. The more they practice, the better they get. Set reasonable expectations for yourself in your area of perceived weakness and work to achieve them. In all likelihood, you'll overcome those known limiting beliefs.

Subconscious limiting beliefs are more difficult to identify because, well, they're subconscious! How do you overcome a limiting belief you don't even know you have? First, you have to identify the belief, which has to be done indirectly. Once again, think of something you're not good at, and if you don't remember when you first learned of that limitation, it may well be that there is a subconscious limiting belief behind it. Alternatively, identify a destructive pattern that has emerged in your life, and there may be a subconscious limiting belief causing you to make decisions that enable your unwanted pattern to continue.

Think back to your childhood. Try to identify an event where you failed at something or where someone may have said something negative to you related to your belief or pattern. If you can't specifically remember someone saying something negative to you, try to imagine a circumstance where that *could* have happened. Let's say, for example, that I'm not very musical, but I don't recall anyone ever outright telling me that. But I can imagine overhearing my piano teacher tell my mother to stop wasting her money! Or perhaps my mother simply stopped the piano lessons when I wanted to continue, and I jumped to the conclusion she did that because I wasn't any good. Any perceived slight or criticism could have caused me to form my negative belief.

In all likelihood, the overarching negative belief you formed as a result of your childhood event was far too broad and all-encompassing. After all, it was just one event, and you were a kid. Let's say you formed the belief that you aren't as smart as other people. But, kids do things all the time that adults think are dumb. If an adult responded and told you when you were seven years old that you were stupid, or that you did something stupid, does that mean you're stupid *now* as an adult? Of course not! That adult probably forgot about the incident almost immediately, and you're still carrying it around all these years later. Forget about it!

Here's a simple three-step process that I have found to be an effective way to get rid of a limiting belief:

1. Identify the specific negative belief or beliefs that are affecting you and connect to the part of you that feels powerless to overcome the negative belief. For example, I felt powerless to overcome the negative belief that I couldn't draw. To me, this was simply a *fact*, not a belief. I had demonstrated my lack of talent many times.
2. Connect with the part of you that has the power and wisdom to help *others*. It's there. You may have felt powerful and wise when you were parenting, teaching, or helping others to cope in difficult times. Recognize the feeling you got in those circumstances and get in touch with it again. For example, I did some teaching years ago when I was in the Navy. I helped students entering the flight-training program who had some deficiencies in their math and geometry education. I helped them pass the Navy's tests in these areas so that they could achieve their dream of flying when they might not otherwise have been able to do so. It made me feel really good. I would say even powerful and wise. When I decided to address the "fact" that I couldn't draw, I looked for that place of power and wisdom within me.

3. Turn that power and wisdom inward. Apply your power to yourself, to change your own negative beliefs, and move forward with a positive pattern. For my drawing problem, I looked at myself as being one of those Navy students from long ago. I advised myself to get some instruction—to find a good book about learning to draw and give it some real effort. Betty Edwards's book was recommended to me (coincidence?), and I soon learned my limiting belief was false.

Apply this process to your own beliefs if you think you may have a limiting belief that says you can't demonstrate psychic abilities. In step 1, the basis for your powerless feeling may be a belief—for example, that only natural-born psychics can demonstrate psychic functioning (and that's not you!). Or you may have the belief that psychic functioning is impossible, or it's crazy, or it's woo-woo stuff that you don't want to be associated with. Maybe you have the fear that you'll be socially outcast as a weirdo if you tell people you have psychic abilities. Whatever it is, identify the specific belief or beliefs that are affecting you in this area.

In step 2, recognize that you have the power and wisdom to help others overcome their limiting beliefs. This parent, mentor, or teacher part of you is usually directed outward, toward others. If you're a parent, for example, you may spend a lot of time encouraging your child and convincing them that they can achieve things that they don't believe they can. For example, convincing them they can make an A in math, or they can become a starter on the school soccer team.

In step 3, when you apply your power and wisdom to yourself, give yourself the same type of pep talk you would give your kid, student, or mentee. And do it *repeatedly* until your negative pattern is broken. Then take some positive action to move forward with a positive pattern. Find a good book with scientific research on remote viewing or other types of ESP to overcome your belief that it's impossible or crazy. I list several such books (such as *Mind Reach* and *The Reality of ESP*) in the bibliography. Then sign up for a remote viewing course so you can experience it yourself. I have taken six remote viewing classes, and in every class, there was not a single student who could not do it. If you're serious about having a psychic experience, just do it!

Here's another way to help get rid of limiting beliefs, especially those that are subconscious. This is more of a meditative process, which I learned in a course called *Duality* by Jeffrey Allen. Allen teaches about the act of using energy to improve your life—earth energy to ground you and provide you with all the energy you need to succeed in your physical body, and cosmic energy to provide the energy you need to succeed spiritually.

In this meditation, you imagine bright white cosmic energy coming down and entering your body at the top of your head (your crown chakra). The energy flows down your back to the base of your spine where it clears out any limiting beliefs in your root chakra (associated with physical survival, health, and money). The energy then moves forward and then up the front of your body, passing successively through the other chakras and clearing out any limiting beliefs associated with them. The cosmic energy clears limiting beliefs from your navel chakra (emotions, sexuality, vitality), your solar plexus chakra (action and personal power), your heart chakra (love for self and others), your throat chakra (communication), your third eye chakra (intuition and guidance), and finally your crown chakra (inspiration and spiritual connection).

The cosmic energy exits through your crown chakra and travels up and away, carrying these limiting beliefs away from you. A great thing about this meditation is that you don't even have to know what the limiting beliefs are. Just know that you are eliminating them. If you have a daily meditation practice, it's easy to add this cleansing meditation to it. You'll know that over time, your most stubborn limiting beliefs are being eliminated, and no new ones can form.

If you have negative beliefs about your psychic abilities, use either or both of the above processes to eliminate them. Discovering your psychic abilities is a great thrill! Don't let what others have said keep you from experiencing this great joy.

You are special. You're committed to learning and being successful. And you want to serve. When you learn this material, you can change your life and other people's lives for the better.

Remember, I was the world's greatest skeptic. If I can do it, so can you! In the next chapter, I'll provide you with some solid evidence to help you overcome your doubts.

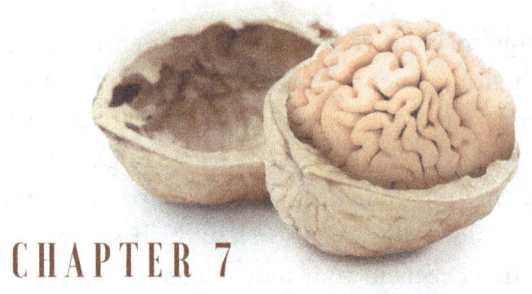

CHAPTER 7

The ESP Experiment That "Opened The Door" For Me

It was a simple experiment that first opened my eyes to the fact that something strange was going on. I discovered, to my absolute shock and amazement, that I was communicating information with other people in a way that couldn't be explained by any known physical means. Here's how it went down.

My friend, Jerry, had been calling me periodically and talking crazy! He was saying that if someone drew something on a piece of paper and then stared at it for a few minutes, that without seeing it, he could meditate for a few minutes and then tell them what they had drawn. I thought he had gone bonkers! He pestered me for months to do an experiment with him, but I conveniently didn't have the time. The weird thing was, Jerry was a genius at designing microprocessors. He owned a company that employed half a dozen electrical engineers. I had drafted and gotten a couple of patents granted for him on his ingenious designs, so his claim to have this telepathic ability was way out of character.

One afternoon, he called me while my girlfriend, Maria, was visiting. Since I wanted him to meet Maria anyway, I finally invited him over to demonstrate his ability to both of us. I figured that even if his demonstration flopped, at least he would have met Maria.

When Jerry arrived, I was a good host and broke out a couple bottles of wine. We sipped away while Jerry regaled us with stories of his successes with his ESP readings. We probably spent close to an hour listening to his stories. He told us it was important for him to tell us about his successes, because it would be critical for our success that we believe *we* could do it. Maybe the wine had some effect, because I found his stories pretty compelling. By the time we got started, I classified myself as a skeptic who was open to the possibility. I was driven by curiosity and the thought that as a science guy, I should always have an open mind. Maria claimed she had no opinion either way. Jerry, of course, was fully convinced his experiment would work.

It wasn't until much later that I fully appreciated just how right Jerry was—how important it is to have the right mindset when you're attempting to do something that you have thought for your entire life was impossible!

We planned an experiment where Maria or I would take turns drawing something on a 3x5 index card, since I had a pack of those handy. They're small enough to hide behind your hands, and they're thicker than paper, too, so a person looking at the back of a card couldn't see what was drawn on the front. As the "transmitter," she or I would stare at our drawing while making sure Jerry couldn't see it. As the "receiver," Jerry was going to meditate for ten minutes or so, make notes or drawings of anything that came to him, and then tell us what he saw through his "third eye," as he called it. With your eyes closed, you can imagine your third eye as being slightly raised and between your eyebrows. After Jerry received, we would trade roles and see if Jerry could mentally transmit a drawing to one of us.

Note also that none of us wore eyeglasses or used reading glasses in those days. We still had young eyes! So there wasn't any way the receiver could see a reflection of the drawing in our glasses.

We agreed that the drawing could be of *anything* we wanted. We didn't want to limit the drawing to one of a few things (like a circle, square, or triangle) because the receiver might just make a lucky guess. The only limitation we put on it was that the drawing had to be something relatively simple. As Jerry explained, if the drawing was too complex, it would be difficult to judge the accuracy of the viewing because the receiver might focus on one aspect of the drawing. For example, if a bicycle was drawn, the receiver might describe a tire or a handlebar or a sprocket or a chain rather than the whole bicycle. So the only limitation on the drawing was that it had to be something simple.

Maria volunteered to transmit to Jerry first and temporarily left the room to draw something on her card. She returned, and we sat together on different sides of my square kitchen table. While she stared at her drawing, Jerry closed his eyes and sat quietly, attempting to open his mind to any messages or images that might enter. I watched carefully to make sure there was no cheating going on and that Maria didn't inadvertently show her drawing or give Jerry any clues. Nobody said anything, and Maria never really moved. She just looked at her drawing. Jerry never looked in her direction or even opened his eyes. I was satisfied there was no way Jerry got any information about her drawing by any normal means.

After ten minutes or so, to my surprise, Jerry became exasperated, grabbed a pen and paper, and made a quick sketch.

"I don't know," he said. "It's like a square, but it's all jumbled up. It keeps shifting around, and I can't get a good picture of it. I give up."

I was surprised at Jerry. After all this buildup, it must have been very difficult for him to concede defeat. I felt sorry for him. On the other hand, I felt relieved that my materialistic world view seemed secure. I figured this was going to be a total failure on Jerry's part.

I asked to see what he drew, and he revealed this sketch of a square with a bunch of lines going every which way around it.

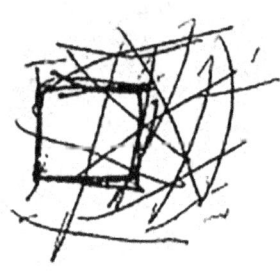

That was a pretty weird drawing. I knew there was no way Maria drew anything like that! I felt smug.

I asked Maria to show us what she drew.

Maria revealed her drawing, which was a transparent (phantom) cube drawn with rough, sketchy lines.

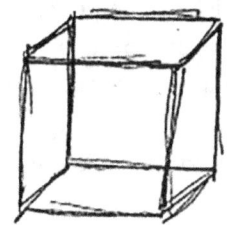

Hmm. Something kind of clicked in the back of my mind. I got the first hint—the first inkling—that my materialistic worldview might be in jeopardy. Despite his crazy drawing, Jerry really hadn't done that badly. He got the square aspect of the phantom cube, and its perspective does shift around. One second you see it from the top right, and the next second you see it from the bottom left. And there were some sketch lines that sort of extended out into space. No wonder it was confusing.

This was intriguing enough to make me excited to continue.

As we talked about it, we decided there wasn't any reason why our future sessions couldn't have one person transmitting and *two* people receiving. We didn't feel we needed anyone to monitor the sessions, and it would give an additional person the chance to participate in each session. I was still glad I had monitored the first session because I had carefully made sure there was no cheating or inadvertent sharing of information. If something drastic was going to happen to my worldview, I didn't want there to be any uncertainty in the process.

For the next session, I was the transmitter, and Maria and Jerry were both receivers. I went out of the room and drew a symbol of the sun—a circle with rays extending out every forty-five degrees. Here's my drawing.

I returned, and Jerry and Maria meditated while I stared at my drawing and made sure neither of them got a peek at it. Once again, Jerry sat quietly with his eyes closed. Maria jotted down notes and made sketches from time to time. After ten minutes or so, Jerry made a quick sketch and then the two of them said they were finished. Jerry went first and revealed his sketch.

I looked at it and was pretty skeptical of whether Jerry was even close this time. I suddenly felt more secure about my worldview after all. It was like I was on a roller coaster and was now headed back up. So I confidently asked him what it was.

And he said, "It's a turbulent, curved surface radiating heat."

I was momentarily confused. That didn't sound like he was describing a drawing. It sounded like he was describing an object—like maybe a portable space heater or something. But then it dawned on me—an object very much like the sun! *That* was a twist I didn't expect! He could be describing the actual sun. If you've seen videos of the surface of the sun, it's churning all over the place, shooting up big geysers of superheated plasma. It's turbulent, curved, and hot!

I desperately clung to my materialistic worldview. My roller coaster was screaming back down, but my worldview was obviously in trouble again. However, I noted Jerry's drawing seemed to be backward. The radiating heat waves seemed to be radiating in the wrong direction. They were radiating toward the center of the sun, not away from it. He had drawn a concave surface rather than a convex one. I realized this thought was out of desperation, but it was a desperate time. (Note: I later learned that remote viewers often flip features of their target from right to left, drawing essentially a mirror image. Something similar may have been going on with Jerry's drawing, especially since he seemed to be remote viewing the sun rather than telepathically describing my drawing.)

I tried not to show any reaction so that I didn't influence Maria's description of what she drew.

So then she revealed her drawing.

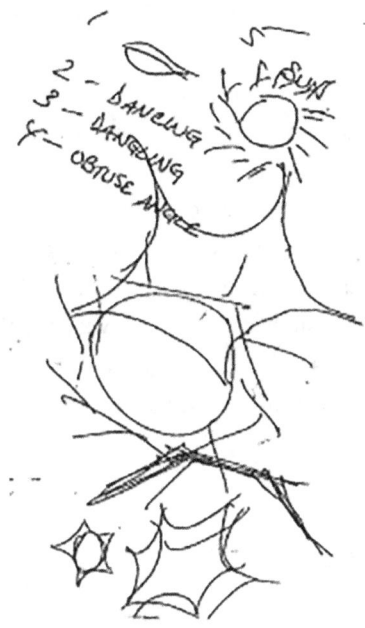

"Whoa, there's a lot there," I said. "Can you tell us about it?"

She said, "I initially got the sense of sunlight filtering and dancing through the leaves of a tree, but then began to concentrate on the sun and the obtuse angles formed by the rays. I numbered the ideas that occurred to me as one through five."

I looked at the sketch and noted at the top she had written the word 'sun' next to a circle with rays extending from it. Getting short of breath, I said, "I see you wrote the word 'sun' next to number five where you drew a circle with rays extending from it. What are the other things below it?"

She said they were all sketches of the sun, and they sort of evolved as time went on.

So then I revealed my drawing of the sun. Everyone was blown away by these results! Jerry got the essence of what the surface of the sun is actually like.

And Maria zeroed right in on my drawing and even wrote the word 'sun' next to a circle with rays extending out from it. Wow!

I was no longer on a roller coaster. I was hanging off the edge of a cliff frantically grasping for small branches to hold onto. But one by one, they were breaking off.

I was in a daze as we moved on to our final session where Jerry made a drawing and transmitted to Maria and me. Jerry left the room with a pen and index card for a couple of minutes and then returned, hiding his drawing. Maria and I started to meditate while Jerry stared at his drawing. This was my only chance to receive, since I had monitored when Maria transmitted to Jerry.

I closed my eyes and tried to clear my mind of any thoughts. I was kind of disappointed because I didn't get much of anything for most of the session. In fact, I was starting to panic because we were running out of time and I could hear Maria writing and sketching almost continuously. How could I have been such a good transmitter but such a lousy receiver? Finally, in the midst of a black void, I saw an image of a roughly triangular form with lights that seemed to be at the ends of booms extending out from each apex. As we ended the session, I made my drawing.

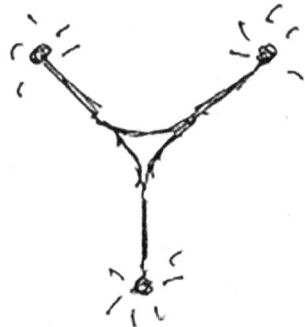

Jerry asked to see mine first. He looked at my drawing and was non-committal. He just said "Hmm," and asked to see Maria's drawing.

Maria revealed her drawing.

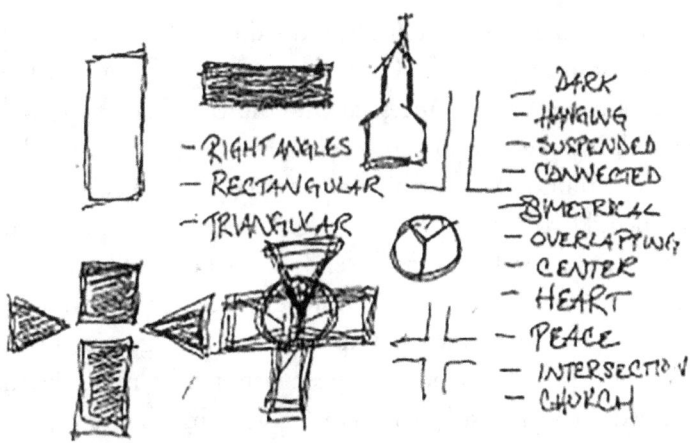

Boy, did I feel inadequate! Maria described how she started out sensing right angles. She thought it might be a road intersection, but it changed to a cross. She drew a peace symbol and a church with a small cross on it. Then she drew some larger crosses that were clearly Christian crosses. She wrote corresponding words, such as "church," "heart," and "peace." Other words, such as "dark," "hanging," and "suspended," could be representative of Jesus's crucifixion.

Then Jerry revealed his drawing.

I jumped up from the table! No way! Having been in the Navy, I started cursing like a sailor. Jerry had been in the Navy, too, and I even had *him* blushing! But after all, my worldview was going up in smoke. It was being obliterated!

It was undeniable that something was going on here. There was some sort of psychic communication between the three of us. I was in shock!

In summary, when you look at our individual performances, you can see that on the transmitting side, all of us had proven to be great transmitters. On the receiving side, our performances varied. I didn't feel I did very well the one time I received. My sketch didn't look much like Jerry's cross. But Jerry noted I did describe certain aspects of his drawing. For example, my sketch had a vertical boom and two booms extending right and left from the vertical boom. It also showed rays extending from the ends of the booms like he drew around his cross. Also, my sketch is typical of how Jesus's body is shown on the cross, with his arms extended outward and upward, and his legs straight down.

Jerry's receiving performance had been better than mine. He had accurately perceived the square shape of Maria's confusing phantom cube and had accurately described the physical characteristics of my sun.

But Maria's grasp of the details was phenomenal! Her sketches were extremely accurate and detailed. She drew a circle with rays extending out from it and wrote the word "sun" for my drawing of the sun. For Jerry's Christian cross, she drew several Christian crosses and a church. She even picked up on the meaning behind Jerry's drawing of the cross, and she had never done this before. She had this incredible ability and never knew it.

Maybe you or one of your close friends does too. In the next chapter, I'll describe how to prepare for and conduct a similar ESP experiment in the comfort of your own home, with the help of a few friends.

After all, the real worth, success, or effectiveness of something can only be determined by putting it to the test—by trying or using it yourself. As they say, the proof is in the pudding. So let's go try it!

CHAPTER 8

Take Off The Blinders And Do Your Own ESP Experiment!

This is an experiment you can do in the comfort of your own home. Just set aside a couple hours of quiet time and get two or more friends to join you—the more the merrier. The more participants you have, the greater the likelihood you'll have someone who does very well. Who knows? One of them may be a natural like Maria. I'm not a natural. I have to work at it and *practice*, but I'm a perfect example that *anyone* can be trained to do it.

The number one rule is: *relax and have fun!*

Here are the materials you will need:

- Blank, unlined white paper for "receivers" to make notes and sketches
- 3" x 5" index cards for the "transmitter" to make his/her target drawing
- Black pens for everyone
- A 10-minute timer
- The description of the experiment described in Chapter 7
- A bottle of wine—optional, but recommended for people with doubts!

The transmitter could also use blank, unlined white paper for the target drawing, but index cards are recommended if the transmitter is going to be at the same table as the receivers. The small cards are easier to conceal and are thicker so the drawing doesn't show through.

You want to make sure all paper is without any lines, markings, or texture of any kind. If using index cards that have lines on one side, the transmitter should make his/her drawing on the unlined side of the cards. Otherwise, the receivers could include the parallel lines in their sketches. Here's an example Jerry told Maria and me before we did our experiment.

Jerry did a session with his wife where her drawing was simply an oval. She didn't have any plain paper handy, so she drew it on a paper dinner napkin, which had a surface texture like small bubbles. In Jerry's session, he perceived an oval shape and small circles. At that point, his analytic mind—that is, the "left side" of his brain—jumped in and interpreted the small circles as bubbles, and interpreted the oval as being the top rim of a champagne glass full of bubbling champagne. So that was his answer. Wrong!

Here's what happened.

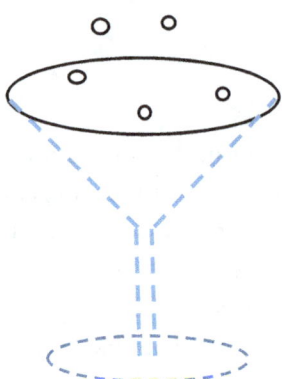

The solid oval and the small circles are what Jerry perceived during the session. Jerry's analytic mind interpreted the small circles as bubbles and added the dotted lines to create an object it recognized. This is a very subtle process, and it's difficult to detect when your mind is automatically doing it. With practice, you'll be able to recognize when it's happening. The biggest clue will be that your description of the drawing includes a *noun*.

If Jerry had said he saw an oval-like shape and some small circular shapes (which is what he actually saw), he would have been exactly right.

Use pens with black ink for all the drawings and notes. Other colors of ink can have subconscious meanings, which may throw you off.

Each session should be about ten minutes. Set a timer if everyone is participating, so you don't have the distraction of watching the clock.

> Pay attention to "set and setting."

A key part of the preparation is to pay attention to the importance of what's called "set and setting." By "set," I mean the *mindset* of the participants. "Setting" refers to the environment where the experiment is conducted.

Mindset

Let's talk first about mindset. As I previously discussed, the number one block in achieving what you want in any area of life is your own negative beliefs. Quite simply, you probably won't succeed if you believe you won't or can't. The reason for this is simple: failure reinforces your negative beliefs. And your mind has a very strong desire to be right.

When I reported for duty at the United States Naval Academy on June 29, 1970, we started an arduous two-month training process called plebe summer. In addition to a lot of physical conditioning, there was a lot of learning and a lot of memorizing to be done, and one of the things we had to memorize was a poem called "All in the State of Mind." I won't bore you with the entire poem, but the opening stanza goes like this:

> If you think you are beaten, you are;
> If you think you dare not, you don't;
> If you would like to win and don't think you can,
> It's almost a cinch you won't.

Don't let your mindset derail you from experiencing one of the coolest things you'll ever see! I just can't tell you how much of a thrill it is when you sit around a table and you see one or more of your friends—or *you*, yourself—demonstrate that you are communicating mind-to-mind. It's absolutely mind-blowing!

> ## Get in the right mindset for the experiment.

So to get yourself and your friends in the right mindset for the experiment, I suggest you show all of the participants the description of the ESP experiment I did with Jerry and Maria. You can download a description of the experiment from my website: www.YouCanLearnTheTruth.com. This is real-life evidence that the three of us communicated mentally. You want to get everyone in the frame of mind where they are open to the possibility that psychic communication is possible. At the very least, they should have no opinion. As long as they don't have a negative opinion, they should be good to go.

Be on the alert for mental conflicts. If you're trying to believe, but in the back of your mind you still believe psychic communication is impossible, your subconscious mind will accept the dominant belief. Remember, that's why we often get the opposite of what we pray for.

One way to overcome a negative belief that psychic communication is impossible is to view more evidence that psychic functioning is real. Read the books I discuss in Chapter 10 about the scientific research that was done on remote viewing at Stanford Research Institute (SRI). Viewers in those experiments described distant target locations with such accuracy that the scientists running the experiments calculated the odds were less than two in a million they could have done it by chance.

The experiments at SRI used more than twenty viewers, and every one of them, even inexperienced viewers, proved they could remote view to some extent. The scientists concluded that remote viewing is probably a latent perceptual ability that is widely distributed in the population.

Note that saying affirmations to yourself such as, "I believe in psychic communication," will generally not work to resolve your mental conflict with an old belief that psychic communication is impossible. What you need is real evidence, and there's plenty of it. And remember, all you need to do is find enough evidence to convince your subconscious mind that there's a *possibility* your old belief was wrong. You don't need to prove it absolutely for your subconscious mind to bring you the results you desire.

You'll probably have the opportunity to find out what your friends think about psychic functioning when you first talk to them about the experiment.

If you find a friend who is dead-set in their opinion that it won't work, I would suggest you find a way to not invite them. You don't want someone there who is going to be voicing his or her negative opinion while others are trying to think positively. One bad apple can spoil the whole bunch.

> *A skeptic in your midst can have an adverse effect on the outcome.*

In fact, research shows that even a skeptical "lurker" (a participant who keeps his negative beliefs to himself) can have an adverse effect on the outcome. The cohesiveness in agreement as to intent within the group (for example, *we will generate great data*) will drive the outcome—along with each individual viewer's intent to be successful. So get everyone to open up and say what they truly believe before inviting them. Doubters be gone!

On the other hand, if you have one of those friends who, as soon as you met them, you felt like you had known them your whole life, be sure to invite *them*! You probably have a strong psychic connection already.

> *If a person has a strong belief, especially one they have an emotional stake in, they will do whatever it takes to prove their belief is correct.*

If you do wind up with a participant who believes it won't work, even if they're trying to believe, it is much more likely they will fail. It's well known in psychology that if a person has a strong belief, especially one they have an emotional stake in, they will do whatever it takes to prove their belief is correct. So their mind will sabotage their effort. Although there have been instances where total skeptics got amazingly accurate results, at this point in your development, you want to have as many factors in your favor as you can.

Drink the wine if necessary! But not too much. We all know a little alcohol can help to release some of our social inhibitions. In the same way, it can help to suspend our disbelief. In my case, hearing Jerry tell about his successes while consuming a couple of glasses of wine, changed my mindset from a pure skeptic (who thought Jerry had gone totally crazy) to one who was open to the possibility that ESP would work.

But obviously, too much alcohol can ruin the experiment. You don't want a bunch of drunks sitting around trying to do ESP. Even if it worked, you might not believe it (or remember it)! Once the experiment begins, put the wine away.

Setting

Okay, that's enough about mindset. Let's talk about setting, in other words, the environment you want to set up for the experiment. Here are some key points:

- Do the experiment when you'll be free from external distractions or commitments for the duration of the experiment. You don't want to be worried about work or the kids or be expecting an important phone call.
- Try to minimize sensory inputs. You want an environment that doesn't create distractions.
- Wear comfortable clothing and sit in a comfortable chair.
- Create as quiet an environment as possible. So don't have music playing or have the TV on in the background.
- Minimize visual distractions. Don't sit where you're looking out a window or looking at a lot of objects sitting on a bookshelf. If you could sit facing a blank wall, that would be ideal.
- Minimize smells. Don't have dinner cooking on the stove, scented candles or incense burning, or have anything else that creates a distracting smell.
- Minimize tastes. Don't eat during the experiment or drink anything other than water.
- Don't do the experiment when you're hungry or when you're uncomfortably full since those sensations can be distracting.

When you're ready to start, isolate the transmitter person. Have the transmitter go well out of sight of the receivers (for example, in another room) to make his/her drawing. No talking by the transmitter! You don't want any possibility that any information whatsoever is passed from the transmitter to the receivers by conventional physical means.

> There's no distance limitation on psychic communication.

When Jerry, Maria, and I did our experiment, we sat at the same table during the sessions and just made sure no clues were given. However, it would be better to have the transmitter out of sight of the receivers. There's no distance limitation on psychic communication, so there's no requirement to sit at the same table during the session. So for an added layer of protection against any kind of physical signaling between the transmitter and the receivers (intentional or unintentional), the transmitter can remain in the drawing-room and merely announce when he/she is ready and starting to stare at the drawing.

The receivers can then quietly meditate for about ten minutes and see what comes to them. Set a timer if everyone is participating so you don't have the distraction of watching the clock.

Now when I say meditate, it's really "meditate" in quotes. It doesn't have to be a deep meditation. We're not trying to reach some altered state of consciousness. Initially, just try to clear your mind of any distracting thoughts or internal dialog. Take a few deep breaths to relax, and then just note any images or words that happen to occur to you during the ten minutes.

You can choose to close your eyes or not. Some may find it more effective to simply look at their blank piece of paper or the tabletop. Maria rarely closed her eyes during her successful sessions. She chose to take her pen and just doodle for ten minutes to see what would show up. Experiment with different techniques to determine what works best for you.

> Describe. Don't identify.

As you meditate, don't try to figure out what the drawing is. Remember Jerry's mistake when he identified his wife's drawing as a champagne glass. In your notes, try not to write nouns. Draw sketches if shapes occur to you, and if you have to use words, use adjectives. *Describe the target drawing, don't identify it.*

The reason for this is that your subconscious mind, which is receiving the information from the transmitter person, does not name things. *Naming* the object is purely a function of your analytical left brain. Your subconscious mind only passes descriptive information, and only a tiny bit of information is trickling from your subconscious mind into your conscious mind. It's not enough information to make an accurate judgment of what the drawing is. Naming what the transmitter drew is just a wild-ass guess, so unless you just get lucky, your guess will probably be wrong.

You should understand at this point that it's not likely that information about the drawing is going to come blasting into your conscious mind. My experience has been that I will write descriptive words and sketch something while having absolutely no idea whether my words or my sketch have anything to do with the transmitter's drawing. It may seem like it's not working, and you're just randomly writing down adjectives and drawing some weird shapes that popped into your mind or that your hand drew without you even knowing what it was doing. It's a very subtle process. Just go with it. If a thought pops into your mind, *write it down.* You'll kick yourself later if you had a thought but didn't write it down and it turns out the thought was accurate.

> **If it's not on the paper, it didn't happen.**

Here's a rule for you: If it's not on the paper, it didn't happen. We're trying to be a little scientific here, and the evidence of psychic functioning has to be on the paper. We can't just take people's word for it when, after the fact, they say, "Oh, I thought of that, but I didn't write it down." No, no, no! That would never convince a skeptic!

Brad thinks I'm NUTS!

> If you go into a session not caring whether you get it right or not, you're more likely to score a higher accuracy.

Don't get stressed out worrying about "getting it right." It may seem counterintuitive, but trying to succeed is counterproductive! Trying to get it right will work against you because your conscious mind will jump in and make guesses, which will probably be wrong. If you go into a session not caring whether you get it right or not, you're more likely to score a higher accuracy. It's an experiment—just draw and write things that pop into your mind. Just go with the flow. Remember the number one rule: *relax and have fun*! It actually helps you get better results.

When time is up, the receivers should keep their descriptions private. One at a time, they should go to the transmitter and explain what they saw. After everyone is finished, get together and have the transmitter reveal his or her drawing. Check out how many aspects of the transmitter's drawing everyone got correct. And don't forget, you may describe aspects of a real object that the transmitter drew, not just the drawing. Remember how Jerry described a "turbulent, curved surface radiating heat" when I transmitted a drawing of the sun.

When you're assessing how you did, don't beat yourself up if your sketch doesn't look like the transmitter's drawing. To gauge your performance, see how many of your impressions correctly described the transmitter's drawing and how many did not. Then you can compute a percentage you got correct.

For example, let's say the transmitter drew a simple rendition of a house—a square with a triangle sitting on top of it. In your session, you sketched a cube. Don't say, "Oh woe is me, I got it all wrong!" In fact, you got it all right! Your sketch includes horizontal and vertical straight lines that intersect at right angles. Overall, your cube is an enclosure. All of those impressions are correct for a drawing of a house. Although you didn't draw a triangle representing a pitched roof, everything you did draw was correct. So while you thought you got it all wrong, you scored 100 percent correct!

Take turns being the transmitter. Some people may be better transmitters than receivers. In my experiment with Jerry and Maria, I was a much better transmitter than a receiver. The result was still meaningful to me since I knew with absolute certainty that neither of them got the slightest glimpse of my drawing or any signals from me. I truly communicated the information from my mind to their minds in some unknown way.

> Don't get discouraged when you have failures. Keep trying. Remember, relax and have fun!

But know this—you're going to have some failures. That's a natural part of achieving *any* goal. You may have a rousing success the first time you do this experiment, but the next three times you try it with other friends, you fail. You'll be disappointed, but don't get discouraged. You're trying to do something you may have thought was impossible—it's a difficult task! But keep trying, and it will change your entire life for the better.

Winston Churchill said, "Success is going from failure to failure without a loss of enthusiasm." Thomas Edison tried over *six thousand* different elements for the filaments in his experimental light bulbs before he found one that would light for more than a few hours without burning out. Jack Canfield and Mark Victor Hansen received 144 rejections from publishers for their book, *Chicken Soup for the Soul* before a small independent publisher in Florida agreed to publish it. It went on to be an international bestseller.

When you have a failure, shrug it off, try to determine what you did wrong, and keep going. Change your thinking from, "I always do this wrong" to "I will learn how to do this right."

Remember, *relax and have fun!* Enjoy the process!

CHAPTER 9

How To Remote View—Your Mind Can Perform Miracles!

I hope you had a roaring success with that ESP experiment. If not, like John Paul Jones said, "Don't give up the ship!" Do it again and again until you have a breakthrough. And remember, the subconscious cues are subtle. Just note any descriptive words or images that come to you, even if they don't make sense. And don't try to put them together into something identifiable. That will mess you up almost every time.

Now, I'll describe for you how to do a simple Remote Viewing experiment that takes the ESP experiment to the next level. Instead of describing another person's drawing, you'll describe a physical object that person has in their possession.

The setup is very similar to the ESP experiment, but instead of a drawing, have the transmitter bring to the experiment, an object such as a pencil, a golf ball, a cup, a piece of fruit, or other simple object hidden in a paper bag or other container that doesn't give a clue about the nature of the object.

When the receivers are ready to begin, the transmitter should say, "I have an object that needs a description."

The transmitter can either stay and keep the object hidden or can leave the room and take the object out of its container and examine it, noting how it looks and feels and smells and so on during the session.

If any of the receivers come into the session with clearly formed initial impressions or images in their minds, they should write them down at the top of their paper and label them as "Initial Images" or "Advance Visuals." Then draw a line under them to separate them from the rest of the session transcript. Otherwise, these initial images will follow the receiver all through his or her session. You know, once you've had a thought about what the object might be, it's difficult to get rid of it! These initial images may or may not have anything to do with the target object.

The receivers should then quiet their minds and start noting all their mental impressions. As a receiver, imagine yourself holding the target object in your hands, and ask yourself whether the object has a color or texture; does it have sharp edges; what could you do with it; does it have movable parts; does it have an odor; is it heavy or light; what does it taste like? Note any sensory impressions that occur to you.

Then look for images of fragmentary shapes or forms. Look for surprising and novel images that you don't normally have in your mental impressions. Make little sketches of these images even though they may not make sense and may not be objects themselves.

> Your objective is to use your subconscious mind and your body as a "dumb" sensor to pick up information about the target object.

Do not name them! Naming and analysis are the principal enemies of remote viewing. To name your images requires your conscious mind to jump in and start analyzing. If a noun occurs to you, it's the result of analysis. Write it down on the right side of your paper and then try to forget about it. Your objective is to use your subconscious mind and your body as a sensor to pick up information about the target object. But you want it to be a "dumb" sensor, that is, a sensor without any processing or analytical power.

It just records descriptions. Remember, the transmitter asked you to *describe* the object, not to identify it.

After noting each new image that occurs to you, take a short break, and remember to breathe. Then look again to see if you are given another image or perhaps the same one with additional information. Again, look for surprising and novel images that you don't normally have in your mental impressions.

The whole process should not take more than 10 to 15 minutes.

When you feel you have written all that you can, take a few minutes to write a summary. Try to distinguish between the images that you feel the most strongly about and those that more likely have originated from noise, memory, analysis, or imagination, or from things you saw earlier in the day. You're trying to separate your most confident psychic bits from the analytical chatter.

When all of the receivers have finished their summaries, the session is over and the transmitter can return to the room and show the object. Compare your summary to the object and note all the correct things you saw in your session. Despite your efforts to forget about nouns that occurred to you during the session, you may have ended up with an impression of what you thought the object was, and if that impression is wrong, you'll likely be disappointed and discouraged. Don't be. Look instead at the descriptors in your summary and note how many apply to the target object. You'll probably be pleasantly surprised!

As with the ESP experiment, it's not likely, when remote viewing, that information about the target object is going to come blasting into your conscious mind. It will probably be much more subtle. It might go something like this example, which I hope will show you how the information might come in, and how you describe the object rather than identify what it is.

Example Remote Viewing Session

As you start your session, you imagine you're looking at the object while holding it in your hands. You write down some descriptive words. Colors may come to you first, and as they pop into your mind, you write down: gold, red, and green. You also think of "shiny" and write that down.

You then imagine how the object feels, and write down hard and metallic. You note the surface feels smooth and then "rough" pops into your mind. You're thinking that's dumb. How can it be both? Am I just doing opposites?

Is my analytic left brain interfering? But maybe it's smooth in one area and rough in another. So since you had the thought, you write it down!

You take another break and then wonder how the object smells and write down "burnt."

        Gold
        Red
        Green
        Shiny

        Hard
        Metallic
        Smooth
        Rough

        Burnt

When no other descriptive words come to you, you decide to sketch something. You should always move down the page as you get new impressions, and you're almost out of room on the first page, so you get another piece of paper and write the number 2 in the upper right-hand corner.

Now let's say before you draw anything, you find your hand making an arcing motion in the air over the paper. So you go ahead and draw your first mark—a long arc, curving over.

                                                                                        2

You take a little break and a deep breath and then see what else comes. This time, without much hesitation, you draw your second mark—another long arc, this one curving under.

2

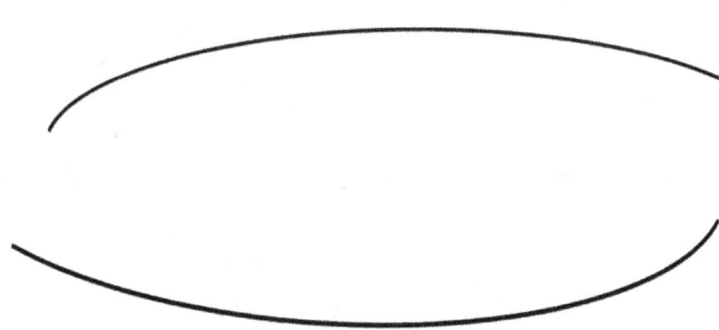

"Hmm," you think. "Did I just draw that because it's sort of the opposite of the first arc? Is my left brain interfering again? Analyzing?" So you take another break and a deep breath.

Then it occurs to you it would be interesting, or even funny, to have a loop at one end of the first arc. So you add a loop.

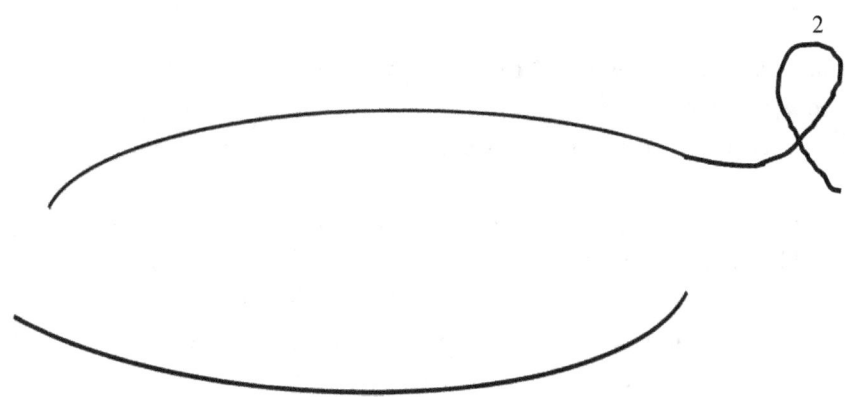

You look at what you have sketched so far, and the idea of a whale comes to mind. Could the object be a toy whale? Then you realize you're making a critical mistake! Your conscious mind is analyzing and making a guess—trying to identify the object with too little information. So you discard the idea of the whale and pause for a few seconds, clearing your mind. When you continue, you draw two vertical parallel lines off to the side. You have no idea why. Right after that, you draw a small oval.

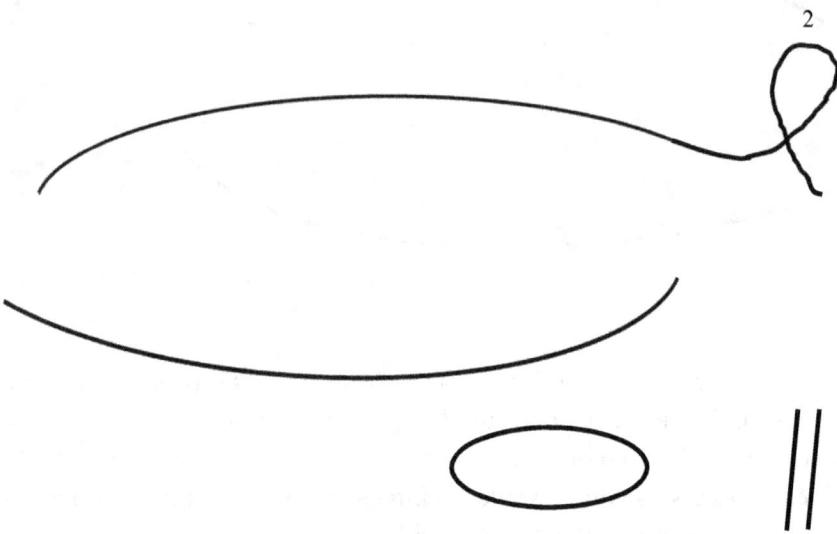

You have no idea how any of these things relate, but it doesn't matter. Your job is to *describe*, not to identify.

No other shapes occur to you, so you write a summary. Your summary says:

> The object is gold, red, and green. The surface is shiny. The object is hard, possibly metallic, and has curved arcs. Something is looping at one end. The surface of the object is smooth and/or rough. A burnt smell is present. The object includes a vertical part and an oval.

As you can see, you haven't identified the object; you have only described it.

When the transmitter returns, she presents you with an Arabian candle holder. You think to yourself, "Wow, I'm sure glad I got rid of that toy whale idea. I would have gotten totally off track if I hadn't!"

Brad thinks I'm NUTS!

As you examine it, you see several aspects that you got correct. Gold and shiny are correct, but the colors red and green are not. The object is hard and metallic, and it has arcing sides and a loop handle at one end. The inside is smooth while the outside is rough because of an etched pattern. And it smells like burnt wax. However, the receptacle that holds the candle is actually round, not oval when viewed straight on, so we have to say the oval, although similar, is technically incorrect.

As for the two vertical lines, they could be representative of an associated candle since your subconscious knows the purpose of the candle holder. But the transmitter did not have a candle in the holder, so by that interpretation, the vertical lines are incorrect. In that case, out of thirteen impressions that you noted, nine were correct. That results in an accuracy of 69 percent. On the other hand, if we note there is a short vertical column that supports the receptacle for the candle, then the vertical lines could be the support column. Then you got ten out of thirteen correct, and that equals an accuracy of about 77 percent.

In either case, you perceived the main features of the candle holder. Not bad for an item that you had never seen and that could have been *anything in the world* small enough and light enough to fit in the transmitter's bag.

> Psychic ability is like musical ability or artistic ability; it's widely distributed in the population, and everyone has some ability and can participate to some extent. The more you practice, the better you get.

As I noted earlier, even the most non-musical person can learn to play a tune on the piano or draw a more realistic image of their hand. The more they practice, the better they get, and the same goes for remote viewing. Remember what I said about my remote viewing classes? *Everyone* had success to some extent. With practice, you get better at differentiating between pure subconscious data and analytical data your conscious mind has generated. That enables you to discard the analytical data, which is usually wrong.

As noted by Russell Targ in *The Reality of ESP: A Physicist's Proof of Psychic Abilities*, the setup of this remote viewing experiment actually provides three possible paths for you, the viewer, to receive psychic data. First is the telepathic connection with your friend, the transmitter, who knows in her mind what the target is. This path is similar to the ESP experiment we did earlier. Second is the direct clairvoyant connection from your mind to the target object. This path is unique to remote viewing and is different from the mind-to-mind telepathic connection. And third is the precognitive connection to the feedback you will receive after you have finished your viewing and the transmitter puts the object into your hand. I'm talking about foreknowledge of the feedback that your subconscious mind has access to even while you're still doing the session.

Wait…what? Yes, you can read your own, future mind!

Here's an example that happened to me. When I attended Joe McMoneagle's remote viewing course at The Monroe Institute, the students sat side-by-side at a large table while we did our sessions. Joe had a stack of numbered large manila envelopes that contained photographs of different target sites. Joe gave each of us a different reference number from the envelopes as our assigned target. For example, he may have walked along the table and said to me, "Your target is 396." Then he might have told the lady next to me, "Your target is 451." And so on.

I did a session where I described a religious structure that included tall columns. When everyone was finished, Joe started handing out the target envelopes with our feedback photos. Before I received mine, he gave an envelope to the lady sitting next to me who promptly opened it, pulled out her target photo, and plopped it onto the table right in my field of view. I couldn't help but see that the photograph was of the Grand Mosque in Istanbul.

Obviously, this is a religious structure with tall minaret columns at each corner. Just like I described. But when I got *my* feedback envelope, it contained a photograph of a waterfall out in the wilderness somewhere. Nothing at all like I described.

> In the realm where your subconscious mind operates, time is not linear.

I called Joe over to look at what had happened and he said, "Hmm . . . she stole your session." He then explained to us how time loops work. In the realm where your subconscious mind operates, *time is not linear*. At the time you're doing your session, your subconscious mind already knows the feedback you're going to receive in the future. But your subconscious is set to report to you the *first* feedback it receives. So when my neighbor student plopped her feedback photo in front of me, my subconscious mind grabbed that image of the Grand Mosque and fed it to me during my session.

Very strange! Think about that one for a while—it's a mind-blower!

However, it doesn't always work that way. The reference number usually leads you to the target, but the reference number I was given seemed to be meaningless in that instance. After all, the reference number was associated with a waterfall. A possible explanation is that my subconscious mind found the mosque to be more interesting, and substituted it.

Here's an example along that line, sure to blow your mind again! In Joe McMoneagle's book, *Mind Trek: Exploring Consciousness, Time, and Space Through Remote Viewing*, he discusses a session he did at SRI in the early 1970s. They didn't use photos in their experiments. They had team members known as "outbounders" drive to a location within thirty minutes of the office in Menlo Park and walk around, observing the area. The viewer back at SRI tried to describe where they were.

In this session, Joe described a multistory building with balconies and hanging plants drooping from the balconies. But the outbounders had gone to a parking lot. Nothing there but asphalt or concrete and maybe a few cars and light poles. His session was recorded as a total miss.

Several years later, Joe flew to California and was driving to the SRI building in Menlo Park. He drove down the street where the parking lot was located and had to pull over to the curb and stare, dumbfounded at what he saw. The parking lot had been replaced by a multistory apartment building complete with balconies and hanging plants drooping from the balconies. The conclusion of the researchers at SRI was that during his session, his subconscious mind had sought out the most interesting aspect of the target site *at any time*, and the apartment building to be built in the future was more interesting than the parking lot at the time of his viewing.

The more you learn about the sessions that were done in the remote viewing studies, the more incredible the subconscious realm and the subconscious mind become. For example, the researchers found that the remote viewing accuracy was even better when the viewer did the session describing the location where the outbounders were located *before* the outbounders randomly drew an envelope from a vault telling them where to go. There's that darn *time* thing again!

Here's a twist on the remote viewing experiment you can do to have some more fun. This procedure ensures that no one's knowledge of the target will interfere with the remote viewing session, and it plays with time in a mind-blowing way!

- Compile a fairly large collection of possible target photos (say, 100 or so).
- Have a viewer perform a session with the intent to "view the target to be selected tomorrow morning" (or later the same day).
- The next morning (or later the same day), have a friend randomly pick four photos from the collection.
- The friend then compares the viewer's session record with the four photos and ranks the photos first through fourth place based on how well each photo matches the session record.
- The friend then *randomly* chooses which of the four photos is the target photo. This means, for example, turn them over, shuffle them, close her eyes, and choose one.
- The friend then provides only the chosen target photo to the viewer and gives him the score (1-4) of the chosen photo.

We did a similar experiment in Joe McMoneagle's remote viewing class, and it worked! Amazing and mind-blowing, but seeing is believing.

CHAPTER 10

What The Heck Is Controlled Remote Viewing (CRV)?

In this chapter, I'll give you a brief overview of Controlled Remote Viewing (CRV), which is an advanced technique you can learn if you want to experience more amazing stuff!

A few years ago, there was a TV series called *The Lowe Files*, where the actor Rob Lowe and his sons traveled around the United States investigating mysteries such as reports of ghosts, the Sasquatch, alien abductions, and so forth. It was light-hearted and somewhat tongue-in-cheek, since they didn't really expect their investigations to turn up anything substantial. It was all in good fun.

In every episode, they came up empty-handed—except Episode 7 of Season 1, which aired on September 13, 2017. In this episode, entitled *Mind Games,* Rob and his sons investigated this "crazy thing" called Controlled Remote Viewing. After a short lesson in CRV by Gail Husick and Paul Smith, one of my former instructors, they tried their hands at it, with *shocking* success. While Rob stayed in the classroom, his sons took the role of outbounders and went to an undisclosed site nearby. As they walked around and noted the architecture and layout of the site, Rob did a CRV session back in the classroom trying to describe the site where they were located—and oh boy, did he! He did it with incredible accuracy. They were all shocked at the result. This time, as they left the filming location and merrily jumped into their SUV, instead of laughing and joking about the fact that they had come up empty-handed again, they were all looking at each other somewhat stunned, as if to ask, "What just happened?"

The series didn't last long, but you can still find episodes online for streaming. *Mind Games* is worth watching.

CRV is a procedure by which one can perceive information not available through the five physical senses that is separated from the viewer by distance, shielding, or time. You may wonder how something as mysterious as remote viewing, with its interconnection with time, can possibly be "controlled", but procedures have been developed for doing this, even though it is not fully understood how the information is transferred.

The CRV protocol was developed over several years in a top-secret government program conducted at SRI in Menlo Park, California. Two scientists involved in the research, Dr. Harold Puthoff and Dr. Russell Targ, were laser physicists who, in the process of researching elementary quantum particles, became involved with an individual from New York named Ingo Swann. Swann had reportedly had significant success with psychokinesis, the process of affecting matter with the mind, and the physicists wanted to study this ability in a controlled experiment. In particular, Swann had demonstrated the ability to affect the readout of a small magnetometer, a compact piece of equipment a foot or so in diameter that measures magnetic field strengths. Puthoff invited Swann to SRI to perform a psychokinesis experiment involving a magnetometer.

When Swann arrived at SRI, he found, much to his surprise (and dismay), that the magnetometer he was to try to influence was an extremely large and sensitive device buried below several feet of concrete and enclosed in multiple protective layers to shield it from magnetic fields, temperature changes, and vibrations. Scientists at SRI and Stanford University used this magnetometer in physics experiments requiring extremely precise magnetic-field measurements made in complete isolation from external influences.

Swann wasn't sure he could do it. He had no idea what the machine looked like, how it was constructed, or how any of its inside coils were aligned. But he agreed to try. Several skeptical physicists from Stanford University observed the experiment and fully expected Swann to fail. But soon after Swann began to concentrate on affecting the magnetometer, the output needle began to move in an uncharacteristic manner. The scientists stopped the experiment, saying they had to calibrate the magnetometer. When they finished their calibration, the experiment continued. Once again, Swann concentrated, and the needle moved uncharacteristically.

A few of the scientists left still skeptical, saying that the magnetometer needed a thorough diagnostic and recalibration. Most, however, including Puthoff and Targ, were amazed. They were convinced Swann had altered the operation of the shielded magnetometer using only his mind.

All of the scientists who used the magnetometer in their physics experiments were horrified! Not because their disbelief in psychic phenomena had been proven wrong, but because the experiment brought into doubt the results of all their prior experiments that had relied upon the absolute isolation of the magnetometer from outside influences. Now it seemed their treasured magnetometer could be influenced by the random thoughts of people walking by!

Dr. Puthoff published a report on the magnetometer experiment and shortly thereafter, "Men in Black" from the Central Intelligence Agency (CIA) showed up at his office door. This was 1972, and the Cold War was still in full swing. The CIA had received some alarming reports indicating that the Soviets were spending large amounts of money researching psychic phenomena. The CIA wanted Puthoff and Targ to perform some experiments investigating whether psychic phenomena were real. The CIA probably would have been very happy if the experiments proved that psychic phenomena were not real, and thus the Soviets were wasting their money. However, they proved just the opposite.

In a book describing their experiments, *Mind Reach: Scientists Look at Psychic Abilities*, Targ and Puthoff state in their preface:

> The primary achievement of this research has been the demonstration of high-quality "remote viewing": the ability of experienced and inexperienced volunteers to view, by means of mental processes, remote geographical or technical targets such as roads, buildings, and laboratory apparatus.
>
> Our accumulated data from over 100 observations with more than 20 subjects indicate the following: The

> phenomenon is not limited to short distances; electrical shielding does not appear to degrade the quality or accuracy of perception; most of the correct information given by subjects is of a non-analytical nature pertaining to shape, form, color, and material rather than to function or name, suggesting that information transmission under conditions of sensory shielding may depend primarily on functioning of the brain's right hemisphere; and finally, the principal difference between experienced and inexperienced volunteers is not that the inexperienced never exhibit the faculty, but rather that their results are simply less reliable. This indicates to us that remote viewing is probably a latent and widely distributed perceptual ability.

Did you get that last part? These two distinguished physicists said their studies indicate that remote viewing is probably a latent and widely distributed perceptual ability. Their studies are well documented. If you're a skeptic, read *Mind Reach*.

Both Targ and Puthoff continued their research into remote viewing and other psychic abilities. In 2012, Russell Targ published *The Reality of ESP: A Physicist's Proof of Psychic Abilities*. Targ includes the results of other research beyond what was done at SRI. Read this book if you're *still* a skeptic. Hey, the numbers don't lie. People simply can't do these psychic things by guessing. They have to be getting information somehow.

Once Targ and Puthoff defined the CRV protocol with the help of Ingo Swann, a top-secret operational unit of psychic spies was set up and eventually ended up under the auspices of the Army Intelligence Command. For years, this unit provided operational intelligence information obtained by remote viewing of targets inaccessible by any other means. Many times, the remote viewers never received any feedback on the accuracy of their information, but since the operational commands kept coming back to them for additional work, they figured their information must have been accurate.

The book *Reading the Enemy's Mind: Inside Star Gate--America's Psychic Espionage Program* by Dr. Paul H. Smith gives a thorough history of the program and its accomplishments. Paul was a remote viewer in the unit and is one of my remote viewing instructors (his website address is included in the bibliography). In the book, Paul tells how, in May 1987, he participated in a CRV demonstration in the Hart Senate Office Building where the Senate Select Committee on Intelligence held classified hearings and received sensitive briefings. The demonstration, which was key for maintaining funding for the Star Gate CRV program, was given to four senior senators: William Cohen (R-ME), Daniel Inouye (D-HI), Warren Rudman (R-NH), and John Glenn (D-OH). Senator Cohen chaired the meeting.

Paul addressed the senators and explained the different roles of the monitor and the viewer in a CRV session. He and his partner, Gabrielle "Gabi" Pettingell, had decided in advance that Gabi would be the viewer, and Paul would be the monitor. Senator Cohen had written down the name of a target of real intelligence interest on a piece of paper, which he had folded and placed out of sight. When Paul and Gabi were ready, he started the session by giving them a target number associated with his target. The session began and Gabi was soon describing an arid, desert landscape with a prominent factory or industrial complex as a focal point. Paul was worried. He was sure she was off because the target seemed too easy compared to the targets they usually did in their operational work. He had expected the senators to give them an especially difficult target.

Gabi went on to describe vile smells, the sensation of danger, and chemicals. Eventually, Senator Cohen said it was enough. All four senators seemed interested in what had transpired. Senator Cohen pulled out the folded paper and revealed that he had written "Rabta, Libya," the name of Qaddafi's secret chemical weapons factory. Gabi had nailed it. The demonstration made Senators Cohen and Glenn avid supporters of the Star Gate program, and on at least one other occasion they strongly voiced their displeasure when skeptical generals tried to scuttle the program.

The number of outstanding results achieved by the psychic spies is too numerous to list. They located crashed Russian planes in Africa, helped with hostage situations, and supported joint counter-narcotics task forces (JTF) in fighting the War on Drugs on both coasts. They provided unique information from remote viewing that enabled JTF forces to solve some of their cases. In a testimonial from someone aware of JTF operations, "Suspects were apprehended and contraband recovered based on Star Gate's remote viewing data."

My favorite achievement of the Star Gate program is a series of sessions performed by Joe McMoneagle, another of my remote viewing instructors. There was a large building at a Russian naval base and none of our intelligence analysts could figure out what was going on in there. Large numbers of workers went in and out of the building each day. The building was located a substantial distance from the water, so the best guess was that the building was being used to develop some kind of new battle tank. Joe remote viewed it, and over the course of several sessions, described more and more detail of an extremely large ballistic missile submarine. Many analysts were skeptical because of the size of the submarine Joe described and the substantial distance of the building from the water. Joe even predicted a launch date for the submarine, and within days of the predicted date, large bulldozers showed up and started digging a canal from the building to the water. They flooded the canal and out came the first Typhoon-class ballistic missile submarine, still the largest submarine in the world.

In the 1990s, because of bureaucratic infighting and disbelief in remote viewing by some members of Congress, the program was defunded. In 1995, news of the program was leaked and was fully described on Ted Koppel's *Nightline* program.

The remote viewing program was later declassified, and all of the former participants in the program were free to discuss it and pursue it as civilians. A number of them did so, as several schools were set up to teach controlled remote viewing. Three individuals who had excellent records as remote viewers in the unit have set up schools, and I have taken remote viewing classes from all of them. The three individuals are Lyn Buchanan (through his protégé Lori Williams), Dr. Paul H. Smith, and Joe McMoneagle. These people are all legit. I have put their website addresses in the bibliography.

There are other schools out there, but I have no experience with them. From their materials, they seem to focus more on what are called "esoteric targets." Those are targets for which you cannot receive any feedback on the accuracy of your information. They include things like events in ancient history, aliens, UFOs, secret bases on the moon, and future predictions. While esoteric targets may be interesting and fun, serious CRV researchers and instructors stick with verifiable targets so viewers can generate accuracy statistics over a large number of CRV sessions.

Lyn Buchanan was a very accurate remote viewer in the psychic intelligence unit. He's not teaching live classes anymore, but he taught a very gifted student, Lori Williams, to teach his methods. She is an excellent teacher and a lot of fun. She teaches live courses online through her company, Intuitive Specialists, so you can take them in the comfort of your home and save on travel expenses, as well. I took CRV Basic, Intermediate, and Advanced courses from Lori, and everyone in her classes did extremely well viewing assigned targets. I highly recommend her classes.

Dr. Paul H. Smith's company is Remote Viewing Instructional Services (RVIS). I took a slightly different version of the CRV Basic course from Paul. Paul is a super-nice guy who runs a tight ship in his courses. He is a tough taskmaster, but you will learn a lot.

Joe McMoneagle teaches at The Monroe Institute in Faber, Virginia near Charlottesville. Joe doesn't teach the CRV method. His method is more of a meditative one because that's how he personally does it. But he teaches the tight controls and protocols that must be used when researching remote viewing. And, he is one of the most famous remote viewers in the world. What a thrill it is to sit and talk to this guy one-on-one! He seems like an ordinary person you would meet on the street but has developed this incredible talent.

Joe was in the Army during Vietnam and injured his back when his helicopter was shot down. He later became an intelligence analyst, and when he was stationed in Germany, he had a near-death experience (NDE), which he attributes to being poisoned. Years later, he had a heart attack and another NDE. I've always wondered whether those NDEs could have contributed somehow to his psychic abilities.

If you want to take advantage of meeting people like Lyn Buchanan, Paul Smith, and Joe McMoneagle, you better hurry. Lyn has retired from live training, but would probably entertain a personal meeting if you asked, because he's such a nice guy. Paul has announced he's retiring in a couple of years. Joe may not be teaching much longer either. So if you want to meet these famous remote viewers, you better get going!

You might also want to check out Lyn Buchanan's book *The Seventh Sense: The Secrets of Remote Viewing as Told by a "Psychic Spy" for the U.S. Military*. You may wonder, *seventh* sense? What happened to the sixth? Lyn's opinion is that we all have a sixth sense that we know and use, but we just haven't consciously named it. That sense is the sense of ambiance. You can easily feel the difference when you walk from a hallway into a business office. Or when you walk off the street into a church or cathedral. Since ambiance is our sixth sense, he contends remote viewing uses a seventh sense.

Lyn says that if you practice your sense of ambiance you will improve your remote viewing ability. Post a little note on every doorway in your house that says, "What's the difference?" This will train you to think about the different feeling (or energy) that every room or hallway in your house has. After practicing the ambiance exercise in my house for a couple of years, I can walk out on my concrete driveway and when I step into the grass, I feel a different energy. If I walk up to a tree and touch its trunk, I feel the tree's energy flowing through my arm, down my side and my leg, and into the earth. This all comes from—yes, you guessed it—*practice*.

Lyn is currently in the process of making a series of videos for online training programs, which will include the full range of remote viewer training from basic through professional. He is also making special applications courses for monitors, analysts, project managers, database managers, and reporters, as well as team-building courses for corporate, military, and service uses. At the time of this writing, courses in CRV-Basic and Associative Remote Viewing are available. Check out his company, Problems>Solutions>Innovations listed in the bibliography.

So let's take a look at the CRV process, referred to as the CRV *protocol*. The CRV protocol requires the viewer to write certain types of information only in defined locations on a blank piece of paper. As the session progresses, the viewer moves down the page like a timeline. This is referred to as the "structure" of the session, and it's designed to keep the left brain (i.e., the conscious analytical mind) occupied while the right brain (i.e., the subconscious mind) receives information about the target and presents it to the conscious mind for writing down. It's kind of like a military unit where the left brain is the general in charge and the right brain is a soldier who has a job to do. The general wants to be in charge and always tell the soldier what to do. By keeping the left brain busy following the structure, it's like keeping the general in his office signing requisitions. With the general out of the way, the soldier can do his job.

The CRV process is actually an interplay between the conscious mind (the general) and the subconscious mind (the soldier). However, the structure helps to overcome one of the major problems in attempts to remote view—the desire to consciously visualize the site. When the viewer attempts to visualize the site, he/she usually stimulates memory and imagination. As the viewer becomes aware of the first few bits of data, there's a largely spontaneous and undisciplined attempt to extrapolate and fill in the blanks. The result is a premature guess on the part of the viewer. For example, an impression of an island may be immediately interpreted as Hawaii; crisscrossing steel girders may be interpreted as a bridge; or a stone wall may be interpreted as a castle. This is called an Analytical Overlay or AOL.

> **Target be damned—structure is everything!**

Making the left brain remember and follow the structure is also why only plain white paper is used. No templates are used to make it easy. Ingo Swann, one of the fathers of the CRV protocol, thought that making the left brain follow the structure was so important, he is quoted as having declared, "Target be damned—structure is everything!"

The CRV protocol is divided into six discrete levels. The levels are called "stages" by some instructors and "phases" by others. I'll call them stages, since that was the original name. Stages 1-3 are generally taught as the Basic CRV course, Stages 4-5 are taught as the Intermediate CRV course, and Stage 6 is taught as the Advanced CRV course. Each course lasts from three to five full days, depending on the instructor, so we'll only be able to look at Stages 1-3 enough for you to get an idea of how the process works.

Each stage is a natural progression that builds on the information received from the previous stage. To learn to remote view, a trainee needs to do practical exercises in each stage until a level of proficiency is reached. Only then can the trainee proceed to the subsequent stage.

In Stage 1, the viewer identifies a major gestalt or classification for the target, such as land, water, or manmade structure.

In Stage 2, the viewer begins collecting descriptive sensory information associated with the target site. The sensory information includes sights, sounds, smells, tastes, textures, temperatures, and energies (for example motion or electrical energy) at the site. The viewer may also perceive dimensional aspects such as long, narrow, sloping, vertical, horizontal, and so on. Any nouns or visual images are noted (at the right-hand side the page) and declared as AOLs.

In Stage 3, the viewer begins to make sketches of the site. The final product of Stages 1-3 (Basic CRV) is the recognition of the overall gestalt and physical configuration of the site.

In Stage 4, the viewer fills out an information matrix having several columns for different types of information. The columns include additional sensory and dimensional information as well as data of an analytical nature. The rows reflect the timeline down the page and show the order in which the viewer perceived the information. The ambiance of the site, such as military, religious, technical, or educational can be expressed. Cultural factors and functional indicators such as power generation, research, or electronic communications can also be reported accurately in Stage 4.

In Stage 5, the viewer uses several tools and special techniques to probe or question the significance of the data produced in the Stage 4 matrix without triggering AOLs.

In Stage 6, the viewer uses a variety of tools to determine specific locations in space and time for the target site. Additionally, materials such as clay, cardboard, building blocks, or poster paper can be used to construct models of specific structures at the site as well as the general configuration of the surrounding area. This modeling is done with "feeling." It is not simply an attempt to render a more exact representation of the site than can be done verbally or by drawing. The kinesthetic activity of modeling appears to both suppress AOL formation and to act as a trigger to produce more detailed information about the site.

I'd like to interject here that the entire time I'm working a CRV session, I have no idea whether the things I'm writing down or drawing have anything to do with the target. When I get my feedback after the session is over, I'm still surprised when I find that my perceptions accurately described the target. When I have a total miss, that is, when I described something completely different than the target, I'm not so surprised. I'm just disappointed. I'm disappointed because I know I let an AOL slip in and didn't notice it. After that, I merely described the AOL.

Some instructors call that "castle building." It's like I perceived the target was a manmade structure, and I perceived a wall made of stone. My analytic mind jumped in and said *castle*! After that, my imagination took over and described watchtowers, a drawbridge, a dungeon, and so forth, when in reality, the target was a fishing pier that happened to have a stone seawall next to it. This is not only frustrating but maddening, since I know I would be a lot better at recognizing AOLs if I practiced more.

In the next chapter, we'll look a little closer at Stages 1-3, and I'll show you some actual sessions I did in my CRV training. This should help you visualize the process better than just words.

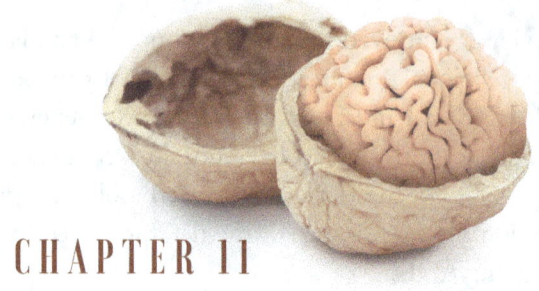

CHAPTER 11

A Deeper, Really Cool Look At CRV Stages 1-3

Let's look at the first three stages of the CRV protocol in a little more detail. Like I said, in a Basic CRV course, you would spend three to five days on these stages, so this is still just a brief overview.

In Stage 1, the viewer attempts to perceive the major classification of the target, such as land, water, or manmade structure. In CRV, this is referred to as the gestalt. Getting the major gestalt(s) is the most important stage in the CRV protocol, since it lays the foundation for everything to come.

Anyone other than the viewer and the monitor (if being used) may assign a reference number called "the coordinates" to the target. When the session begins, the viewer writes down the coordinates and immediately begins a process referred to as the I-A-B process. "I" refers to an "ideogram," a primitive squiggle the viewer quickly draws in response to writing the coordinates. "A" is a step where the viewer first describes the sense of motion and direction that the viewer experienced while creating the ideogram on the page, and then touches the ideogram to determine how it feels. "B" is more or less a wild-ass guess as to the major gestalt represented, although some instructors say you can train your subconscious mind to provide specific ideograms for related gestalts.

Brad thinks I'm NUTS!

> The first time I saw a viewer draw an ideogram, I thought it was the most ridiculous thing I had ever seen!

The ideogram, which is drawn spontaneously without thinking about it, is produced by the subconscious mind, and it captures the overall feeling/motion of the gestalt of the site (e.g., fluid/wavy for water). The viewer should note how the ideogram felt as they drew it.

The first time I saw a viewer draw an ideogram, I thought it was the most ridiculous thing I had ever seen! The viewer repeated a number out loud as he wrote it down, and then immediately drew a squiggle to the right of the number. I wondered, "*That's* supposed to contain information about the target?" It seemed crazy, but it works.

CRV instructors say the squiggle is caused by a signal from the target impacting the viewer's nervous system. Just as the viewer finishes writing the coordinates, he places his pinpoint on the paper and keeps his arm relaxed so that when the unconscious, almost imperceptible impact is experienced, the pen produces the ideogram on the paper.

In step A, the viewer describes the motion of the ideogram by describing the sense of motion and direction that the viewer experienced while creating the ideogram on the page—for example, looping back, curving around, angle down, and so on. He then touches the ideogram to see how it feels—hard, soft, fluid or liquid, airy or gassy, squishy, and so on. The feeling refers to the consistency of the gestalt. For example, a manmade structure may feel hard while a liquid like water may feel fluid. The shape of the ideogram, combined with the motion and the feel, is a symbolic representation of the gestalt created by the viewer's subconscious mind.

In step B, the viewer guesses the major gestalt represented. The viewer has to take care not to rely only on the way the ideogram looks. For example, a wavy line might represent rolling hills if the line feels hard but might represent water if the line feels liquid. Some instructors teach that each individual has his/her own unique ideograms for each major gestalt such as land, water, manmade structure, airiness, energy, or biological. They say that with practice, you can learn to recognize the symbols your subconscious mind is using for each gestalt. Other instructors reject this kind of lexicon approach and insist each target will produce a unique ideogram. Regardless of the approach taken, ideograms remain a mysterious and fascinating way to identify the essence or gestalt of a target.

Here's an example of a Stage 1 session from my Basic CRV course. This is what I wrote on the paper:

>   STEVE SMITH
>   AUSTIN, TX
>   1/25/11
>   3:31 pm.
>   NANCY
>
> 110125001 ⌒‾   A. rising up
>   peaking
>   sloping down
>   across
>   solid
>
>   B. LAND

At the top right is the session information including name, location, date, time, and the name of my monitor for the session, Nancy. The number 110125001 is the coordinates for this target. As soon as I finished writing the coordinates, I immediately let my hand draw the ideogram. In the "A" section, I described the motion I felt while drawing the ideogram—rising up, peaking, sloping down, and across. I then noted how it felt: solid. In the "B" section, I made my guess as to the major gestalt represented. I said it was land.

And here was my feedback, showing that the target was Death Valley, California. Clearly land.

― Brad thinks I'm NUTS! ―

During my Basic CRV training, however, I probably had more Stage 1 misses than hits. For example, I guessed water for one of my sessions, but the target was an office building in Arlington, Virginia. Obviously not water! When this happens, the secret is to not get discouraged. Just keep practicing.

Most real-world target sites contain multiple types of targets and will generate multiple ideograms strung together in a combination ideogram. For example, if the target is at a shoreline, there will be both water and land present at the site. When you recognize multiple ideograms in the squiggle, just repeat the A and B steps for each one.

Once the gestalt or gestalts have been identified, the viewer moves to Stage 2 and begins to write down sensory information associated with the target site. The sensory information includes sights, sounds, smells, tastes, textures, temperatures, and energies at the site. Any nouns or visual images are noted and declared as AOLs.

To do Stage 2 well, you must have a broad vocabulary of adjectives describing each of the five physical senses as well as dimensional words. You're trying to describe what your senses would experience if you were physically at the target location. If you don't have the vocabulary, it doesn't matter how much accurate information your subconscious provides. If you can't describe a scene that is physically in front of you, you can't expect to describe one that is not.

Here's an example of one of my CRV sessions through Stage 2. There are 4 pages.

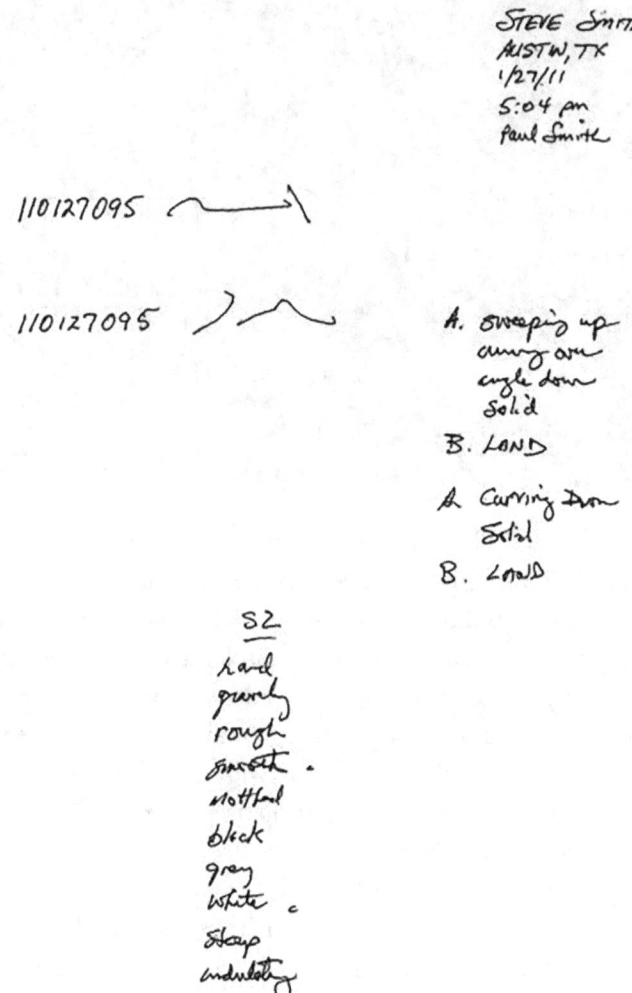

On page 1, after writing the session information, I wrote the coordinates and did an ideogram, but I didn't like the way I did it. I felt like my conscious mind was controlling it. So I wrote the coordinates again and drew a different ideogram. I determined there were two ideograms in a combination, so I did two A-B sections, each one resulting in a *land* gestalt. I then started Stage 2, denoted by the S2 heading. I wrote several sensory indications including hard, gravely, rough, mottled, steep, undulating, gray, black, and so forth. I then moved to page 2.

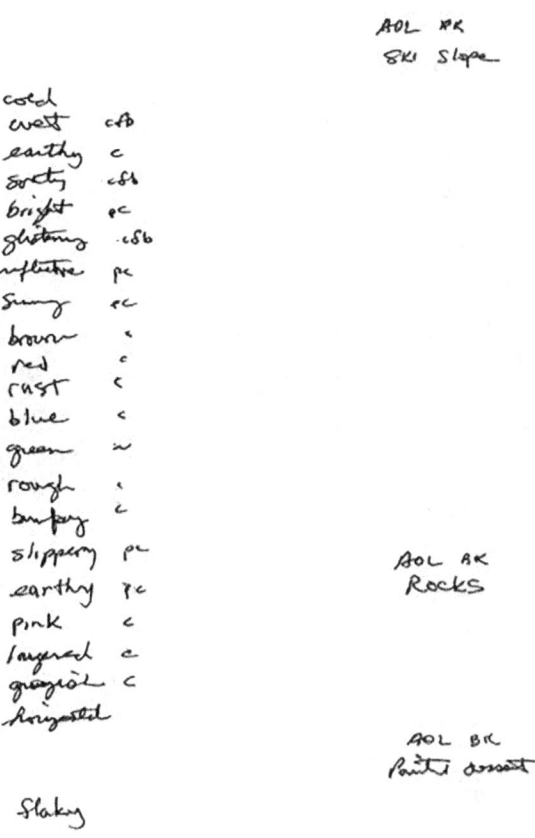

On page 2, I continued to list sensory information like earthy smells; colors like brown, red, rust, blue, and green; some tactile feelings like bumpy and slippery; and some dimensional information like layered and horizontal. I also noted the day was bright and sunny. The little abbreviations you see after some of my entries are just grading marks, so don't worry about them. I also noted several AOLs in a column on the right. At various times, I wrote "ski slope," "rocks," and "painted desert." I then moved to page 3.

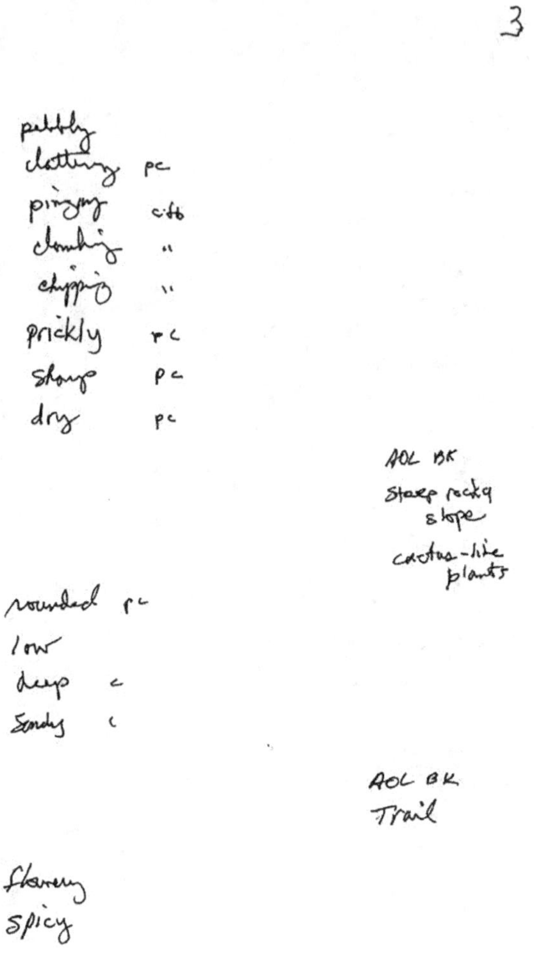

3

pebbly   pc
clattering   pc
pinging   c/b
clanking   "
chipping   "
prickly   rc
sharp   pc
dry   pc

AOL BK
Steep rocky slope
cactus-like plants

rounded   pc
low
deep   c
sandy   c

AOL BK
Trail

flowery
spicy

On page 3, I continued to list tactile feelings like pebbly, prickly, and sharp; some sounds like clattering, pinging, and clanking; and more dimensional information like rounded, low, and deep. I noted several more AOLs, like "steep rocky slope," "cactus-like plants," and "trail." I then moved to page 4.

On page 4, I sensed I wasn't getting any additional information, so I looked back over the information I gathered in Stages 1 and 2 and wrote a summary. You may find that some of the information you gathered during the process seems to be contradictory. At this point, however, you have enough information to put together a summary describing major aspects of the target.

> Summary: The target is land rounded and rocky with a steep rocky slope. Loose gravel. Sunny day with clear blue sky. Rocks are layered with red, pink, brown, gray, and black. Possible clattering noise.

My summary said, "The target is land rounded and rocky with a steep rocky slope. Loose gravel. Sunny day with clear blue sky. Rocks are layered with red, pink, brown, gray, and black. Possible clattering noise."

So now I waited for my feedback. My instructor handed me a folder labeled with the coordinates for this target. I opened it and saw this photograph of Bryce Canyon, Utah.

Wow! Pretty accurate although I omitted from my summary a lot of other information that was also accurate, like "sandy" and "prickly, sharp, cactus-like plants."

Near the end of Stage 2, the viewer may get a series of dimensional descriptors, such as sloping, large, rounded, steep, and so on, and these may result in the viewer having what is referred to as an Aesthetic Impact (AI). At this point, the viewer can write down how the target makes him/her feel—for example, interested, curious, excited, apprehensive, and so forth. It is then time to move to Stage 3 and begin sketching the target.

Like the good vocabulary needed in Stage 2, you need to be able to sketch well to do Stage 3 properly. Practice your sketching by selecting nearby objects and drawing them. If you can't accurately draw something physically sitting in front of you, you can't expect to accurately draw something 1,000 miles away.

When you begin sketching, you may feel that you are just totally making stuff up. You have no idea what you're drawing—you just let your pen move around the paper and see what it draws. Other times, you very definitely start to draw something immediately recognizable. You need to make sure here that you're not following an AOL. You may want to take a mental break and start another drawing. Never discard anything from a session. Merely move down the paper and start another drawing.

Here's an example of one of my CRV sessions through Stage 3. There are 5 pages.

———————— Brad thinks I'm NUTS! ————————

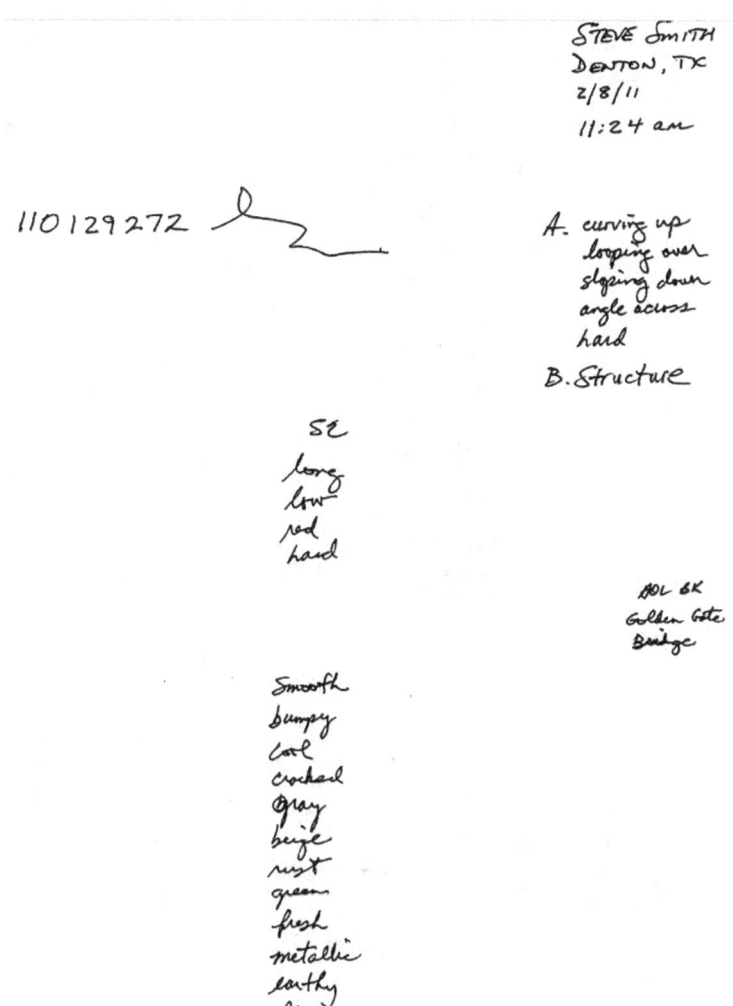

On page 1, following the session information, I wrote the coordinates and did an Ideogram. As you can see, the I-A-B process led me to guess it was a manmade structure. I began Stage 2 and wrote several sensory impressions. I noted an AOL of the Golden Gate Bridge. After writing some additional sensory impressions, I moved to page 2.

On page 2, I continued to list sensory impressions. Following a series of dimensional descriptors—vertical, angled up, angled down, horizontal, and extended—I did an AI break (BK) and noted how I felt about the target—interested, curious, and a feeling of vertigo. I then started a Stage 3 sketch. This looked like some sort of building with a horizontal portion and a vertical portion like a tower. So I moved to page 3.

———————— Brad thinks I'm NUTS! ————————

3

AOL BK
Lighthouse

AOL BK
AIRPORT
ROTATING
BEACON

Bright
Shiney
rotating
luminescent

On page 3, I decided to see if I could get more information about the top of the tower. My sketch was very reminiscent of a lighthouse, so I declared an AOL of a lighthouse or an airport rotating beacon. I then noted some additional sensory indications of bright, shiny, rotating, and luminescent. I then moved to page 4.

4

On page 4, I drew another sketch concentrating on the perceived horizontal portion of the structure. I drew steps leading to a door in the center, and windows on each side of the door. I described the area around the structure as soft in some places and hard in others.

When I sensed I wasn't getting any additional information, I moved to page 5 and wrote a summary.

5.

Summary: Target is a structure that is hard and smooth. A vertical portion seems to be shiny and luminescent, especially at the top. Perhaps intermittent or rotating. A horizontal portion extends from the vertical portion and is low compared to the vertical portion. There appears to be a curved, soft area adjacent to the horizontal portion with a hard perimeter.

My summary said:

> Target is a structure that is hard and smooth. A vertical portion seems to be shiny and luminescent, especially at the top. Perhaps intermittent or rotating. A horizontal portion extends from the vertical portion and is low compared to the vertical portion. There appears to be a curved, soft area adjacent to the horizontal portion with a hard perimeter.

So then my instructor gave me my feedback. Point Loma lighthouse, California.

Amazing! My sketch of the horizontal portion was very accurate, with stairs leading up to a door in the center, and windows on each side of the door. My vertical portion was also accurate except that I drew the tower at one end of the building instead of the center. However, there was another building adjacent to the lighthouse that could give the overall impression of the tower being near one end of the combined buildings. There also appears to be soft ground with a hard perimeter (a fence) although the fence is straight rather than curved. Overall, not bad for having absolutely no information about my target other than a reference number!

As a final CRV example, I'll show you the summary from a session I did through Stage 6. This is the summary of my "final exam" in the Advanced CRV course. I was given the coordinates (reference number) for the target and was told only, "The target is an event. Describe the target." I worked on the target for a couple of days and made this clay model toward the end:

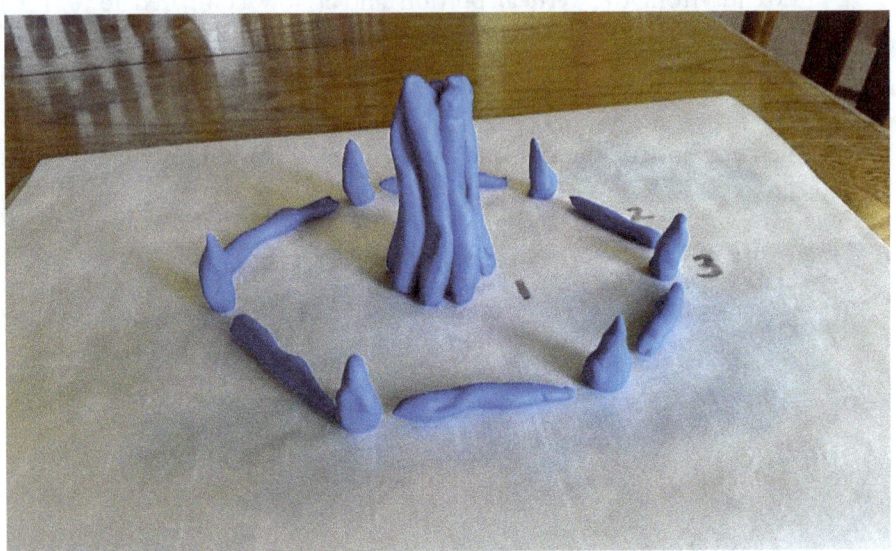

As I molded my clay, I first made a number of clay logs. Then I took several of them and bunched them together to form a vertical cylinder, which I described as being something manmade. The logs lying on the ground in a circle represented a security area keeping a large number of people away from the manmade cylinder, which I sensed was emitting light and heat. The bullet-shaped knobs between the logs represented security personnel.

I then wrote a 3-page summary.

―――――――――― Brad thinks I'm NUTS! ――――――――――

[Handwritten notes:]

24

Summary

Summary Overall 49/60 = .82

The target is an event that elements of:
- manmade ✓
- motion/energy ✓   4/4 = 1.0
- bio/organic ✓
- land ✓

The target is an event involving a vertical manmade with a surrounding boundary that is guarded. There are multiple people who may be celebrating or honoring with light and heat. The event may have occurred between 1712-1725.

Manmade is or has:
- Wooden   N
- hard   Y
- metallic   Y
-   Smooth   Y
-   mottled   N
- old   N   11/15 = .73
- red   Y
- green   N
- cylindrical Y
- horizontal Y
- vertical   Y
- large   Y
- sharp   Y

On the first page, I noted that the target is an event that includes elements of manmade, motion/energy, bio/organic, and land. The "elements" in the summary reflect four gestalts I determined in Stage 1. The summary states:

> The target is an event involving a vertical manmade with a surrounding boundary that is guarded. There are multiple people who may be celebrating or honoring with light and heat. The event may have occurred between 1712-1725.

I then proceeded to list sensory information that was noted in the earlier stages of the session. The sensory information is listed for each of the gestalts. Then I moved to the second page.

```
Defensive      y
Protective     y

Motion/Energy is or has:
Light          y
  bright       y
  flash- short duration  M
Heat  Red, orange, hot   y
Rattling                 y
Clanking                 y
booming                  y

Bio/Organic is or has:
Human – multiple    y
  – guards          y
Red        y
black      y
green      N
orange     N
blue       y
soft       y
mushy      y
earthy     N
warm       y
moist      y
brown      y
beige      y
```

$7/7 = 1.00$

$16/19 = .84$

On the second page of the summary, I continued to list sensory *and analytical* information such as defensive and protective. I noted there are multiple people, some of whom are guards. I described the motion/energy as including bright light and heat that is red, orange, and hot. Rattling, clanging, and booming can be heard. Finally, I moved to the third page.

Brad thinks I'm NUTS!

26

```
Happy           Y
Entertained     Y
Confident       Y
Competitive     Y
Afraid          Y

The land is or has:
 Rocky          Y
 Rough          Y
 Sloping        Y           3/6 = .50
 Vertical       N
 Sheer          N
 high-cliff     N

The space/air is or has:
 Outdoors       Y
 warm           Y
 breezy         Y           6/6 = 1.0
 High           Y
 Vertical       Y
 I feel small   Y

Other things I perceived at the target:
 nighttime      N                        2/3 = .67
 people were gathering to honor or celebrate.  Y
 Fire was involved.    Y
                              Session end
                                1209
```

On the third page of the summary, among other things, I added another gestalt of space/air and said the event was outdoors. It was warm and breezy. There was something high and vertical, and I felt small. Additionally, I noted that the people at the event are variously happy, entertained, confident, competitive, and afraid.

My instructor then revealed my event.

The Apollo 11 launch and mission to the moon. Wow! I felt great about this although some of my information was wrong. For example, the technique I used to establish the date of the event didn't work this time. I said the event occurred between 1712 and 1725, while it was actually July 16-24, 1969. However, I did accurately describe many other aspects of that Saturn 5 rocket launch. It was certainly a vertical manmade cylindrical object. There was bright light, red and orange heat, and booming at the time of the event. It was a warm day with thousands of happy and entertained spectators being kept away from the launch pad by security guards and fences. It's also reasonable to presume that some members of the NASA launch team and the Apollo 11 crew were confident, competitive, and perhaps a little afraid.

You may have noted a Y or an N next to the listed impressions in my summary. After receiving my feedback, I graded my performance by noting (Yes or No) whether each impression in my summary was present or not at the target event. My overall score was 49 correct out of 60 impressions. That means that without any up-front information about my target event, I was 82 percent accurate describing an event that occurred 900 miles away from where I did the session, and almost 50 years in the past.

How can that be? How does this work? How can the human mind retrieve information so distant in both space and time? I'll tell you about some theories in the next chapter.

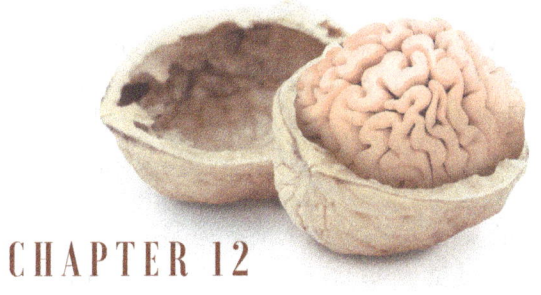

CHAPTER 12

Scientific Theories Explaining Psychic Functioning

In Chapter 1, I told you I would cover some of the latest theories about how psychic functioning works, put forth by experts in the field. This discussion gets a little heavy in the details of quantum physics. So if that doesn't interest you, you can skip to Chapter 13, where, for those of you who want to pursue expanded consciousness further, I'll provide you with some recommended next steps.

1. We're Living in a Computer Simulation

Do we really want to seriously consider physicist Tom Campbell's Big TOE theory that we're living in a virtual reality—that is, a computer simulation? What you have to realize is that if his theory is correct, it would be virtually impossible to detect proof with our physical senses. Tom has devised some variations of the double-slit experiment that could force the universe to present inconsistent results, and thereby prove we're in a simulation, but he has to find an optical physics lab that will agree to do them.

If we, in fact, live in a future society that has refined virtual reality to the point that users cannot distinguish a computer-generated virtual reality from physical reality, and we are plugged into a virtual reality machine that enables users to experience lives in the distant past, then we may be experiencing this life as entertainment or as a history lesson. We could be like Arnold Schwarzenegger when he takes a virtual reality vacation and winds up embroiled in espionage on Mars in *Total Recall*.

> The probability that we're in a computer simulation is not as unlikely as you might think.

What's the probability that we're in a computer simulation, being fooled by computer-generated inputs to our brain that mimic sensory data? It seems pretty unlikely, but it's not as unlikely as you might think.

Professor David Kyle Johnson, Ph.D., Associate Professor of Philosophy at King's College, produced a course for "The Great Courses" called *Exploring Metaphysics*. Dr. Johnson points out that our mental activity is 100 percent generated by and dependent upon the activity of the neurons in our brains. All of our senses, all thoughts, and all beliefs are reactions to what we experience. Future technology could accurately mimic sensory signals to the brain, and an "experience machine" could create an entire world for you and me to experience. Further, he points out, we don't really know if we are carbon-based beings at all. The wiring and firing of our brains could be duplicated on a powerful Artificial Intelligence (AI) computer. We don't know how the firing of neurons in our brains gives rise to consciousness, so we can assume the exact same firing sequence on a computer would produce consciousness. The sensory signals that we receive would convince us that we have real carbon bodies and live in a physical world.

Dr. Johnson further states that the probability that we live in a computer simulation is directly proportional to the probability we will develop the technology for experience machines. Why? If we assume there is a physical universe, then there are two possibilities: an advanced experience machine of sufficient sophistication is never developed anywhere, or such machines *are* developed. If we develop the technology, we can presume it will become widespread, just like smartphones today. There will be billions of such machines in the physical world. So how would we know which possibility we are in—the one with no experience machines, or the one with billions of experience machines?

To answer that, imagine you're in a dark room where there are one billion people and one billion hats. One of the hats is red and the rest are blue. Everyone grabs a hat in the dark and puts it on. What color is your hat? Well, the chance of it being red is only one in a billion, so it is probably blue. Likewise, if there are billions of simulated worlds and only one physical world, we are probably in a simulated one.

So the key question is, what is the probability that we develop this advanced experience machine? Dr. Johnson points out there are five possibilities:

1. We never reach that technology level (or destroy ourselves before we get there).
2. Ethical considerations prevent the development of such a machine.
3. We lose interest or put our resources toward projects in other areas.
4. Technological limitations make it impossible.
5. We do it.

Since it's practically a certainty that if we do it, we are in a computer simulation, then the overall probability of being in a computer simulation is 20 percent (i.e., 1/5), assuming an equal chance that each of the five possibilities could come to pass. That's probably much higher than you thought!

Detractors say the whole idea is ludicrous. Think how enormous a system would have to be to simulate the billions of galaxies in the universe, the billions of stars in each galaxy, and the billions of planets circling those stars all the way down to the quantum particles that make up their individual atoms. A total impossibility for any civilization to develop.

> The system doesn't have to simulate the entire universe. It only has to simulate the sensory inputs to our brains.

But the fact of the matter is, the system doesn't have to simulate the entire universe. It only has to simulate the sensory inputs to our brains. In other words, the system needs only to project onto our perception bubbles, the sensory information necessary for us to experience the world around us.

For example, if I'm standing on a riverbank and I look upstream and see a waterfall in the distance, the system does not need to fully simulate the waterfall. At this point, it only needs to create a video of a waterfall and present it to me. As I walk closer to the waterfall, my perspective changes and the system makes the waterfall appear taller and wider. Also, the system may add sound when I get close enough to hear the roar of the water. When I arrive at the waterfall and reach out to touch the falling water, it is only then that the system must send my brain tactile inputs simulating the feel of real water. Note also that the system does not have to simulate the quantum particles and individual atoms of the water because my five physical senses cannot perceive matter at that level. It's only when I'm doing experiments in the physics lab to measure quantum particles that quantum particles must be simulated.

Likewise, if I look through a telescope and see a distant galaxy, the system only has to present an image of the galaxy to my perception bubble. The system does not need to simulate the billions of stars and planets in that galaxy, not to mention the quantum particles and atoms of that galaxy, because the galaxy is too far away for me to ever get there and observe them more closely.

Remember also, being in a computer simulation provides a nice, tidy explanation for quantum entanglement. Those entangled particles that instantly transmitted information between them weren't really miles or light-years apart—they're just simulations on the same hard drive. So quantum entanglement doesn't violate relativity's speed-of-light limitation after all.

One last point. As we discussed back in Chapter 5, two objects can't be less than a Planck length apart, and two events can't be separated in time by less than a Planck time. So at the very smallest scale, the physical universe is laid out in an array of these tiny little space/time pixels. On the smallest scale, the physical universe is digital. Why would that be, if the universe is not computer-generated? Certainly makes you go "Hmm."

Another explanation of the digital universe is that the reality we experience is not created by an advanced civilization; it's created by God. In other words, God is creating the physical realm so that we can experience physical lives, and the discovery of these tiny space/time pixels provides a hint as to how He's doing it. The question of whether or not that's true is, as we used to say in the Navy, above my pay grade. I'll leave that up to you to decide what you believe.

———————————— Brad thinks I'm NUTS! ————————————

> In a computer simulation, psychic functioning does not violate any principles of physicalism.

So how does living in a computer simulation explain psychic functioning? In such an environment, all of our sensory information comes from the controlling computer. If I'm doing a remote viewing session, the computer knows the target and feeds me relevant information describing the target. No principles of physicalism are violated. My mind does not have to mysteriously connect the coordinates with the target, and it doesn't have to collect descriptive information from hundreds of miles away and many years in the past. All of the information is resident on the same hard drive. If the computer operator wants me to have a successful session, she programs the computer to send me accurate information. If she wants me to fail, she programs the computer to send me inaccurate information.

Nevertheless, to most of us, it's rather unsatisfactory to conclude we're in a computer simulation. So let's look at some other possibilities.

2. Nonlocal Events and Quantum Entanglement

Are we able to perceive a distant event because the quantum particles that make up the atoms of our brains are entangled with quantum particles located at the event? Or can we communicate subconsciously with our friends because the quantum particles that make up the atoms of our brains are entangled with quantum particles in our friends' brains?

ESP skeptics who don't know anything about physics are fond of saying that ESP can't be real because it would violate the laws of physics. That is not true. The evidence shows that we live in a nonlocal universe. To quote Professor Mark Fox in his 2010 Oxford University graduate text *Quantum Optics*:

> The non-locality implied by the quantum interpretation of the Einstein-Podolsky-Rosen experiments has no counterpart in the classical world. The measurement of the state of one photon instantly determines the results for the other one....

The implication is that microscopic systems that are non-local exist in nature.

The physics of non-locality is fundamental to quantum theory. The most exciting research in physics today is the investigation of what physicist David Bohm calls quantum-interconnectedness, or nonlocal correlations. The idea was first considered by leading physicists in the 1930s as evidence of a defect in quantum theory. Einstein famously called this apparent quantum-interconnectedness of entangled photons "spooky action at a distance."

> **No theory of reality compatible with quantum theory can require spatially separate events to be independent.**

Nevertheless, quantum-interconnectedness was later formulated in 1964 as a mathematical *proof* by John Stuart Bell, whose nonlocal (distant) correlations have now been experimentally demonstrated in laboratories all over the world. But the mathematical proof known as Bell's Theorem does not have to be demonstrated in the laboratory. It is not a conjecture, a theory, or a supposition. Rather John Bell gave us a mathematical *proof* that our space-time reality is nonlocal—whether we like it or not. As noted earlier, it appears that entangled photons are affected jointly by what happens to each twin, even many kilometers away. Similar quantum experiments have been carried out with photons, electrons, atoms, and even 60-carbon-atom Buckyballs. Bell further emphasizes, "No theory of reality compatible with quantum theory can require spatially separate events to be independent."

Physicist Henry Stapp of the University of California at Berkeley states that these quantum connections could be the "most profound discovery in all of science."

Let's look at some other evidence of nonlocal connections. Here's an interesting optical experiment.

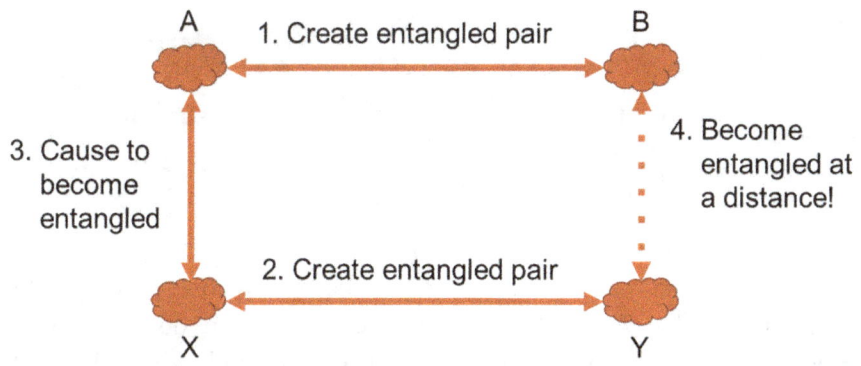

In step 1, entangled photons are created by shining a laser with energetic, short-wavelength violet light into a non-linear crystal. This gives rise to two new entangled lower-energy, deep-red photons, which we can call A and B. In step 2, two more twin photons are similarly created, which we can call X and Y. At step 3, if photon A from the first set of twins and photon X from the second set of twins are brought together and caused to become entangled, their widely separated twin brothers B and Y, through the miracle of non-locality, also become instantaneously entangled, even though they never came anywhere near one another.

Regarding psychic abilities, one theory says that such abilities arise from the fact that the atoms of our brains consist of subatomic particles that are enmeshed in what is called the nonlocal quantum realm. There is even substantial evidence for nonlocal connections between *human* twins. As described by Russell Targ in his book, *The Reality of ESP*, one famous set of twins, reared far apart from birth, were confusingly both named Jim. Although they never communicated, each twin married a (different) woman named Betty, divorced her, and then married a (different) woman named Linda. When the twins finally met for the first time when they were 39 years old, they discovered they had both decided to be firemen, and both had felt a compulsion to build a circular white bench around a tree in their backyard just before they met. This would certainly appear to be a *human* nonlocal connection.

> There's a striking similarity between the nonlocal functioning of remote viewing and the description of nonlocal optical experiments in the physics laboratory.

The view of many quantum physicists is that we live in a nonlocal reality, which is to say that we can be affected by events that are distant from our ordinary awareness. That's the evidence. No one presently knows how *ESP* works, but there's a striking similarity between the nonlocal functioning of remote viewing and the description of nonlocal optical experiments in the physics laboratory.

But when we remote view, we perceive information distant in *time* as well as space. For example, I remote viewed the Apollo 11 launch 50 years after it occurred. And in an earlier chapter, we discussed time-loops between remote viewing sessions and the feedback photos. So non-locality seems to also run through time.

Take this interesting example from an experiment by Daryl J. Bem, a psychology professor at Cornell University. He ran two sets of memory tests in which participants tried to recall lengthy lists of words. In one set of tests, the participants never saw their word list again after completing the memory test. In the other set of tests, the participants were briefly shown their word list a few seconds after they completed the test. Surprisingly, showing the word list to the participants *after* they completed the test significantly improved their memory of the words *during* the test. The future improved the past. In other words, going over the correct answers to a test after you have taken the test can improve your grade!

It's clear that we don't understand how we are bound up in this thing we call time, but it does affect our psychic functioning, and time-shifting of information may affect our daily lives in ways we don't currently comprehend. There is no doubt that we have contact with the future in a way that shows, unequivocally, that we misunderstand our relationship to the dimension of time we take so much for granted.

3. The Universe is a 4-Dimensional, Space-Time Hologram

Is the whole universe, in some way, enfolded in everything, and each thing enfolded in the whole?

In physics, quantum mechanical wave functions predict and describe with perfect precision (10 decimal places in optics) what we will experience in our physical measurements. The wave functions are solutions arising out of the Schrödinger equation, which is the quantum mechanical engine used to solve all problems in the quantum domain. However, the solutions are usually treated as merely mathematical models, so-called probability waves.

> We're all embedded in a physical, 4-dimensional, space-time hologram.

Physicist David Bohm contends, however, that these wave functions make up a physical, 4-dimensional, space-time hologram in which we are all embedded. In Bohm's interpretation, the quantum mechanical-wave functions are treated as having measurable effects through space and time. These wave functions describe what Bohm calls "active information," and this information has its own nonlocal existence.

Here's an easier way to picture some of this esoteric quantum-level stuff. I like *easy* if I can do easy!

As you may know, a hologram is a special kind of three-dimensional photograph that is created with lasers. A laser beam is split into two, and one split beam shines directly on a holographic plate. The other split beam bounces off an object you want to make a hologram of and then onto the holographic plate. The laser beams interfere with each other and create an invisible optical interference pattern that's spread throughout the plate. When you illuminate the plate with a laser beam, you see a three-dimensional image of the object that was photographed. But if you look at the plate without the laser, the embedded three-dimensional image is invisible. It is entirely dispersed in the invisible optical interference pattern spread throughout the plate. The image is there, but you can't see it or any evidence of it. Bohm calls this the "implicate" or enfolded order in the holographic plate. The "explicate" order would be the three-dimensional picture that you see when you illuminate the plate with a laser beam.

> **Each piece of a hologram contains all of the information of the whole hologram.**

Another characteristic of a hologram is that if you take it and break off smaller and smaller pieces, the three-dimensional field-of-view decreases along with the spatial resolution, but you still get the whole picture. In other words, if I have a hologram with a nice clear three-dimensional image, and I accidentally drop it and break it, I can pick up a piece of that hologram and shine a laser on it and still see the *entire* three-dimensional image. It will just be smaller and fuzzier. Each piece of the hologram contains all the information of the whole hologram.

The important idea here, regarding Bohm's interpretation, is that each of us has our mind in our own piece of the 4-dimensional, space-time hologram. And that piece contains *all* the information that has ever existed in the universe.

Bohm says, "The essential features of the implicate order are that the whole universe is in some way enfolded in everything, and that each thing is enfolded in the whole." This is the fundamental statement of a holographic ordering of the universe. It says that, like a hologram, each region of space-time contains information about every other point in space-time, and *experiments have shown that this information is available to consciousness.* That's why we can remotely view events 50 years in the past and 900 miles away.

Note that the holographic universe theory also explains how an entangled quantum particle *instantly* reacts when its twin particle is measured many miles away. The information doesn't have to travel faster than light between the two particles. The information about each particle is always available to the other particle since each piece of the universe contains all of the information of the whole universe.

Bohm rejects any kind of mind-body duality. There is no real division between mind and matter, psyche and soma. The common term *psychosomatic* is, in this way, seen to be misleading, as it suggests the Cartesian notion of two distinct substances in some kind of interaction.

In the holographic universe, there is a unity of consciousness: a greater collective mind with no boundaries of space or time. Remote viewing reveals to us a part of our spiritual reality, but it is only a tiny part of the total spiritual spectrum.

So, is David Bohm's interpretation universally accepted by physicists? Heck no! But what new theory is? Accepting that the sun is the center of the solar system took 2,000 years. Remember what I said earlier: science advances funeral by funeral. The old guard is going to hold onto their beliefs for dear life.

But I applaud David Bohm for coming up with a theory that supports *all* the data. Not just laboratory data about photons, but also laboratory data about remote viewing results and ESP results, which I know from personal experience are as real as any photons.

> You only have to retrieve data from your local piece of the universe, and your subconscious mind has continual access to that information.

A short answer to the question, "How is it that I can psychically describe a distant object?" is that the object is not as distant as it appears. You only have to retrieve data from your local piece of the universe, and your subconscious mind has continual access to that information. The data from thousands of remote viewing sessions suggest that all of space-time is available to your consciousness, right where you are.

Remember back in Chapter 3 when I told you how the volunteers in the psychedelic experiments who received the Psilocybin wandered around the chapel exclaiming they were *one* with the universe? We kind of laughed at them, didn't we? Well guess what? The latest thinking in physics says *they were right*!

Elephant in the Room

The elephant in the room here, of course, is the question of how our minds become aware of information that resides in entangled quantum particles or that resides in a particular part of a holographic universe occupied by our minds. The information is there and our minds are there, but how do we access it? How is it that this information is available to consciousness?

World-class remote viewers will say no one knows. But we may know soon.

Biophysicists are currently researching how the structure and activity of our brains give rise to consciousness. Research into structures such as microtubules is revealing that these tiny structures have quantum properties and communicate with cells using three different layers sensitive to kilohertz (kHz), megahertz (MHz), and gigahertz (GHz) frequencies. Further research is needed, but these tiny structures, only as long as 22.5 nanometers, may hold the answer. Stay tuned. Or better yet, get an advanced degree in biophysics and find out!

CHAPTER 13

Where Can You Go From Here?

I f I've piqued your interest, here are some next steps you can take in your own pursuit of expanded consciousness.

If you have not tried the ESP experiment, do it!

If you have tried the ESP experiment and the results were inconclusive or negative, do it again! As I mentioned, even the most experienced people in the world have failures. *Let go of the need to succeed* and try it again. Just relax and go with the flow.

Try the experiment as a remote viewing experiment with an object in the transmitter's possession instead of a drawing. There are more pathways for you to receive the target information when remote viewing.

Review the remote-viewing example in Chapter 9 showing how the psychic information of the Arabian candle holder might come in. Remember, this is descriptive information, not identifying information. Don't feel like you failed if you were not able to identify the transmitter's drawing or object. Look at each descriptor you wrote down and see if it is present in the target drawing or object. Your accuracy might surprise you. In the example of the Arabian candle holder, the sketches and descriptive words did not identify what the object was, but the accuracy was about 77 percent. That's very good for an object that you had never seen and that could have been *anything in the world* small and light enough to fit in the transmitter's bag.

I cannot overemphasize the importance of the set and setting. Of the two, mindset is more important than the environment. You and your other participants must at least be open to the possibility that it will work. Note that in the experiment I did with Jerry and Maria, neither Maria nor I had ever done an ESP experiment before. I was somewhat skeptical, but Jerry had convinced me there was a *possibility* that it would work. Maria was noncommittal but open to the possibility. In that experiment, I was able to successfully transmit to her a symbol of the sun. So review the experimental results in Chapter 7—and perhaps my CRV sessions in Chapter 11—to reinforce that you *can* be trained to perform ESP (telepathy) and remote viewing.

Go to my website: YouCanLearnTheTruth.com. There you will find:

1. A link to my online course, "The Reality of Psychic and Spiritual Experiences: How an Aerospace Engineer Learned the TRUTH and How You Can, Too." Some people are visual learners, and they learn better by watching videos than they do by reading a book. If that's you, you could benefit from watching my course.
2. A bibliography listing the various books and courses mentioned in this book.
3. A description of the successful ESP experiment from 1996. Review this with your participants to help shift their mindset to one open to the possibility that ESP is possible.
4. A useful checklist for preparing for and conducting your ESP experiment.
5. A meditation audio to help you release limiting beliefs.
6. A useful blog full of information that will help get you on the path to success.

Learn to meditate and do it daily. Check out different meditation techniques and find one that works for you. As I mentioned, I took a course in Transcendental Meditation, a mantra-based meditation technique, which teaches that you should meditate for twenty minutes twice a day. TM was remarkably effective at enabling me to quiet my mind. By alternating meditation and activity during my day, I was able to experience a new type of consciousness in my daily life.

―――――――――― Brad thinks I'm NUTS! ――――――――――

Take the Gateway Voyage course from The Monroe Institute in Virginia. You can purchase CDs or MP3 audios from the institute and listen to them at home, but if at all possible, I recommend going to one of their five-day, six-night residential courses on-site in Virginia.

Read the three related books by TMI founder Robert Monroe: *Journeys Out of the Body*, *Far Journeys*, and *Ultimate Journey*. These books are fascinating! Monroe's initial fear when he started having out-of-body experiences and his subsequent engineer-like method of studying them make these books very credible.

Take a remote viewing course given by one of the former members of the Army's psychic intelligence unit. The ones I've listed in the bibliography are the real deal. They're good, and they can be trusted.

If improving your *spiritual* awareness is your primary goal rather than developing *psychic* abilities, then daily meditation is the most important step you should take. Make it a habit. Like brushing your teeth. Schedule it into your daily routine.

My experience was that mixing daily meditation with the teachings of The Monroe Institute transformed me from an atheist to a believer in an absolute God of pure love that oversees the universe. In the course of just a few months, you can come to know your true spiritual nature and begin to feel the all-powerful, ever-present energy source that pervades everything. Call it Divinity, or Source, or God, or All That Is, or any other name you like—you will sense its unconditional love.

Discovering your subconscious mind and learning to use its unlimited power is an important part of the human experience. You may believe you only live once and then cease to exist, or you may believe you only live once and then go to either heaven or hell. Or you may believe you have an eternal soul that lives hundreds of human lives learning and absorbing life's lessons as you evolve toward a reunification with God. Regardless of your religious beliefs, why would you want to miss experiencing this critical aspect of your existence? I'll answer that for you—*you don't!* Get out there and do it!

I sincerely hope you benefited from this book even more than you dreamed possible. Keep practicing and you'll get better and better. Discovering your psychic and spiritual powers can change *everything*! It did for *me*, and it can for *you*.

EPILOGUE

You'll recall that in Chapter 1, I told you I had two reasons for writing this book. First, I want to help people who have never had a psychic or spiritual experience discover the truth as I did. Second, I want to improve the sad state of the world we live in by showing people that we are all connected, thereby creating a shift toward a more peaceful, caring world.

But as I spent many months drafting and redrafting this manuscript, I began to realize I have a third reason for writing this book. I'll be 68 years old by the time this book goes to press. My days of flying fighter jets, working as a radar engineer, and drafting high-tech patent applications are over. I feel I contributed to humanity in each of those professions, but how can I continue to contribute during my remaining time? In this day and age, I could easily live another twenty-five or thirty years. How could I just sit around and enjoy the fruits of my labor for that long, while people out there need help?

In a way, perhaps this third reason is a little more selfish than my first two reasons. Yes, I still want to help others, but this reason has an element to it that's self-serving. I want to help others so I'll feel good about myself as I approach the end of my life on this planet. I'll feel that I wasn't selfish for my last thirty years. I suppose it's an issue we all have to face as we approach our transition from the physical to the spiritual realm. After all, we're all going to die. We're all on the same train headed to the same station. Is it that bad to want to be proud of all you accomplished?

In the latter part of Johann Sebastian Bach's life, his fame as a composer faded as classical music displaced his baroque style. But instead of fading into obscurity, he spent much of the last ten years of his life writing *The Art of the Fugue*. He wrote it to pass on the techniques of the baroque to later generations. Perhaps he felt a little as I do. He couldn't contribute any longer in the way he had when he was young, but he *could* still contribute by passing on his knowledge and experience. In this way, he could be proud of what he did in his later years.

I'm convinced that teaching about my experience as a science guy who awakened to his spiritual nature can help other people, particularly those who are skeptical, uninformed, or who are struggling with their faith. I sincerely hope, regardless of your particular state of mind, that this book has helped you in your development as a human being and your exploration of what that means.

EPILOGUE 2

What? *Two* epilogues? How many times have you seen a book with two epilogues? Never, I'll bet. Until now.

But it occurred to me that you science guys out there were probably reading this book and the whole time you were thinking, "Okay, this is really cool stuff, but when is he going to talk about *Star Trek*?" After all, how could a science guy like me write a book, *any book*, and not mention *Star Trek*? So to make sure I'm not disappointing anyone, here are some quotes from several of the *Star Trek* series and movies that I enjoy. They show some of the deep philosophical thinking that was going on while those brave men and women went where no one had gone before.

From ***Star Trek: First Contact***

> I am the beginning, the end . . . the one who is many. I am the Borg.
> —Borg Queen

From ***Star Trek: The Next Generation***

> For that one fraction of a second, you were open to options you had never considered. *That* is the exploration that awaits you . . . not mapping stars and studying nebula . . . but charting the unknown possibilities of existence.
> —Q, "All Good Things . . ."

Pulaski: To feel the thrill of victory there has to be the possibility of failure. Where's the victory in winning a battle you can't possibly lose?
Data: Are you suggesting there is some value in losing?
Pulaski: Yes. That's the great teacher. We humans learn more often from a failure or a mistake then we do from an easy success.
—"Elementary, Dear Data"

From *Star Trek: Deep Space Nine*

Ah! An open mind: The essence of intellect.
—Garek, "Past Prologue"

I'm no writer, but if I were, it seems to me I'd want to poke my head up every once in a while and take a look around . . . see what's going on. It's life; . . . you can miss it if you don't open your eyes.
—Sisko, "The Visitor"

From *Star Trek: Voyager*

Without the darkness, how would we recognize the light?
—Tuvok, "Cold Fire"

From *Star Trek: Beyond*

Spock: Ambassador Spock has died.
McCoy: Oh Spock, I'm sorry. I can't imagine what that must feel like.
Spock: When you have lived as many lives as he, fear of death is illogical.

From *Star Trek: The Original Series*

Now, I don't pretend to tell you how to find happiness and love, when every day is just a struggle to survive. But I do insist that you *do* survive. Because the days and the years ahead are worth living for. One day, soon, man is going to be able to harness incredible energies—maybe even the atom—energies that could ultimately hurl us to other worlds in some sort of spaceship. And the men that reach out into space will be able to find ways to feed the hungry millions of the world and to cure

their diseases. They will be able to find a way to give each man hope and a common future. And those are the days worth living for . . .
—Edith Keeler, "The City on the Edge of Forever"

And, of course, I would be remiss if I didn't include a little *Star Trek* humor. Here's one of my favorites from **Star Trek: The Next Generation**.

Alien hologram impersonating Captain Rice: Tell me about your ship, Riker. It's the *Enterprise*, isn't it?
Riker: No, the name of my ship is the *Lollipop*.
Captain Rice (Hologram): I have no knowledge of that ship.
Riker: It's just been commissioned. *It's a good ship.*
—"The Arsenal of Freedom"

> Remember the number one rule for ESP and remote viewing experiments:
>
> *Relax and have fun!*

BIBLIOGRAPHY

Books

Abbott, Edwin A. *Flatland: A Romance of Many Dimensions.* Mineola, NY: Dover Publications, 1884, 1992.

Brown, Courtney. *Cosmic Voyage: A Scientific Discovery of Extraterrestrials Visiting Earth.* New York, NY: Penguin Group, 1996.

Buchanan, Lyn. *The Seventh Sense: The Secrets of Remote Viewing as Told by a "Psychic Spy" for the U.S. Military.* New York, NY: Simon & Schuster, Inc., 2003.

Buhlman, William. *Adventures Beyond the Body: How to Experience Out-of-Body Travel.* HarperCollins e-books, 2018.

Buhlman, William and Susan. *Higher Self Now! Accelerating Your Spiritual Evolution.* New Charleston, SC: CreateSpace, 2016.

Castle, Nathan G. *Afterlife Interrupted: Helping Stuck Souls Cross Over.* Fluid Creations, Inc., 2018.

Dossey, Larry. *Healing Words: The Power of Prayer and the Practice of Medicine.* New York, NY: HarperCollins Publishers, 1994.

Edwards, Betty. *Drawing on the Right Side of the Brain.* New York: St. Martin's Press, 1989.

McMoneagle, Joseph. *Mind Trek: Exploring Consciousness, Time, and Space Through Remote Viewing.* Charlottesville, VA: Hampton Roads Publishing Company, Inc., 1993.

Monroe, Robert A. *Journeys Out of the Body.* Garden City, NY: Anchor Press/Doubleday, 1977.

Monroe, Robert A. *Far Journeys.* New York, NY: Doubleday, 1985.

Monroe, Robert A. *Ultimate Journey.* New York, NY: Doubleday, 1994.

Pollan, Michael. *How to Change Your Mind: What the New Science of Psychedelics Teaches Us About Consciousness, Dying, Addiction, Depression, and Transcendence.* New York: Penguin Books, 2018.

Roberts, Jane. *Seth Speaks: The Eternal Validity of the Soul.* San Rafael and Novato, CA: Amber Allen Publishing and New World Library, 1972, 1994.

Smith, Paul. *Reading the Enemy's Mind: Inside Star Gate—America's Psychic Espionage Program.* New York, NY: Tom Doherty Associates, LLC, 2005.

Smith, Steven Ware. *An Adventurous Soul: One soul's exciting journey through the Human Learning School.* www.amazon.com, 2019.

Targ, Russell and Putoff, Harold E. *Mind-Reach: Scientists Look at Psychic Abilities (Studies in Consciousness).* Charlottesville, VA: Hampton Roads Publishing Company, Inc., 1977.

Targ, Russell. *The Reality of ESP: A Physicist's Proof of Psychic Abilities.* Wheaten, IL: Theosophical Publishing House, 2012.

The Holy Bible, Revised Standard Version.

Walsch, Neale Donald. *Conversations with God, An Uncommon Dialogue, Book 1.* New York, NY: G.P. Putnam's Sons, 1996.

Yogi, Maharishi Mahesh. *Science of Being and Art of Living: Transcendental Meditation.* New York, NY: Penguin Group, 1995.

Courses

Allen, Jeffrey. *Duality.* www.Mindvalley.com.

Buchanan, Lyn. Online Courses: *CRV-Basic* and *Associative Remote Viewing.* Problems>Solutions>Innovations. http://crviewer.com

Gateway Voyage. www.MonroeInstitute.org.

Johnson, David Kyle. *Exploring Metaphysics.* www.thegreatcourses.com.

Lifelines. www.MonroeInstitute.org.

McMoneagle, Joseph. *Remote Viewing.* www.MonroeInstitute.org.

Our Incredible Journey: Life, Death and Beyond. William and Susan Buhlman. www.MonroeInstitute.org.

Serving Spirit. www.MonroeInstitute.org.

Smith, Paul. *Controlled Remote Viewing-Basic.* Remote Viewing Instructional Services. rviewer.com.

Transcendental Meditation. www.tm.org.

Williams, Lori. *Controlled Remote Viewing-Basic, Intermediate, and Advanced.* IntuitiveSpecialists.com.

Williams, Lori. *Controlled Remote Viewing, Medical Applications.* IntuitiveSpecialists.com.

Articles

Griffiths, R.R.; W.A. Richards; U. McCann; and R. Jesse. "Psilocybin Can Occasion Mystical-Type Experiences Having Substantial and Sustained Personal Meaning and Spiritual Significance," *Psychopharmacology* 187, no. 3 (2006): 268-283. doi: 10.1007/s00213-006-0457-5. [Discussed in Michael Pollan's book, *How to Change Your Mind*, listed earlier.]

ABOUT THE AUTHOR

STEVEN WARE SMITH is a true science and engineering guy who grew up being a total skeptic about psychic phenomena. After graduating with honors from the U.S. Naval Academy with a degree in Aerospace Engineering, he flew fighter jets in the military for eight years and then worked as a radar systems engineer for seven years. He returned to school at the University of Texas School of Law, and afterwards worked as a patent attorney for 26 years specializing in high-technology telecommunications patents. In 1996, he participated in an ESP experiment that was so successful it awakened him to his latent psychic powers. Subsequent study and experience convinced him that *anyone* can learn to demonstrate psychic functioning. He now teaches people how to discover their psychic abilities and thoroughly enjoys the look of astonishment when students experience their first successful psychic event.

Learn more at www.YouCanLearnTheTruth.com.

www.ingramcontent.com/pod-product-compliance
Lightning Source LLC
Chambersburg PA
CBHW051402290426
44108CB00015B/2123